HARD QUESTIONS

ABOUT

HUMANITY

Only A. Guy

Hard Questions about Humanity
Copyright © 2015 by Only A. Guy All rights reserved.
Published 2015

Published by VIP Ink Publishing, L.L.C. | www.vipinkpublishing.com
Book Layout by Gershom Reese Wetzel | www.aoristos.com

For information about special discounts for bulk purchases, please contact VIP Ink Publishing, L.L.C. special sales department at business@ vipinkpublishing.com

First Edition Print

ISBN-13: 978-1-939670-19-9
ISBN-10: 1939670195
Printed in the USA.

Hard Questions About Humanity

1. Question:
"What is Christian Anthropology?"

Answer: Anthropology is the study of humanity. Christian Anthropology is the study of humanity from a Christian / biblical perspective. It is primarily focused on the nature of humanity - how the immaterial and material aspects of man relate to each other. Here are some common questions in Christian Anthropology:

What does it mean that man is made in the image and likeness of God (Genesis 1:26-27)? The image of God refers to the immaterial part of man. It is that which sets man apart from the animal world, fits him for the "dominion" God intended (Genesis 1:28), and enables him to commune with his Maker. It is a likeness mentally, morally, and socially.

Do we have two or three parts? Are we body, soul, and spirit - or - body, soul-spirit? Human beings were intended to have a relationship with God, and as such, God created us with both material and immaterial aspects. The material aspects are obviously those that are tangible and only exist as long as the person is alive. The immaterial aspects are those which are intangible: soul, spirit, intellect, will, conscience, etc. These characteristics exist beyond the physical lifespan of the individual.

What is the difference between the soul and spirit? It is important to understand that both refer to the immaterial part of man, but only the "spirit" refers to the man's walk with God. The "soul" refers to man's walk in the world, both material and immaterial.

What is the origin of the different races? The Bible does not explicitly give us the origin of the different "races" or skin colors of humanity. In actuality, there is only one race - the human race. Within the human race, there is vast diversity in skin color and other physical characteristics.

Christian Anthropology deals with who we are and how we relate to God. Whether people are inherently good or inherently sinful is crucial in determining how our relationship with God can be restored. Whether the souls of human beings carry on after death determines in large part our view of our purpose in this world. Christian Anthropology helps us to understand ourselves from God's perspective. When we delve into this subject, we get a clearer understanding of our fallen nature, and this leads to a sense of wonder at the love of the Savior who saw our helpless state and went to the cross to redeem us. When we accept that sacrifice and appropriate it as our own, our natures are transformed by God who creates in us a completely new person (2 Corinthians 5:17). It is this new person who can relate to Him as we should, as His adored children.

A key verse on Christian Anthropology is Psalm 139:14, "I praise you because I am fearfully and wonderfully made; your works are wonderful, I know that full well."

2. Question:
"Do human beings truly have a free will?

Answer: If "free will" means that God gives humans the opportunity to make choices that genuinely affect their destiny, then yes, human beings do have a free will. The world's current sinful state is directly linked to choices made by Adam and Eve. God created mankind in His own image, and that included the ability to choose.

However, free will does not mean that mankind can do anything he pleases. Our choices are limited to what is in keeping with our nature. For example, a man may choose to walk across a bridge or not to walk across it; what he may not choose is to fly over the bridge—his nature prevents him from flying. In a similar way, a man cannot choose to make himself righteous—his (sin) nature prevents him from canceling his guilt (Romans 3:23). So, free will is limited by nature.

This limitation does not mitigate our accountability. The Bible is clear that we not only have the ability to choose, we also have the responsibility to choose wisely. In the Old Testament, God chose a nation (Israel), but individuals within that nation still bore an obligation to choose obedience to God. And individuals outside of Israel were able to choose to believe and follow God as well (e.g., Ruth and Rahab).

In the New Testament, sinners are commanded over and over to "repent" and "believe" (Matthew 3:2; 4:17; Acts 3:19; 1 John 3:23). Every call to repent is a call to choose. The command to believe assumes that the hearer can choose to obey the command.

Jesus identified the problem of some unbelievers when He told them, "You refuse to come to me to have life" (John 5:40). Clearly, they could have come if they wanted to; their problem was they chose not to. "A man reaps what he sows" (Galatians 6:7), and those who are outside of salvation are "without excuse" (Romans 1:20-21).

But how can man, limited by a sin nature, ever choose what is good? It is only through the grace and power of God that free will truly becomes "free" in the sense of being able to choose salvation (John 15:16). It is the Holy Spirit who works in and through a person's will to regenerate that person (John 1:12-13) and give him/her a new nature "created to be like God in true righteousness and holiness" (Ephesians 4:24). Salvation is God's work. At the same time, our motives, desires, and actions are voluntary, and we are rightly held responsible for them.

3. Question:
"Who was Cain's wife? Was Cain's wife his sister?"

Answer: The Bible does not specifically say who Cain's wife was. The only possible answer is that Cain's wife was his sister or niece or great-niece, etc. The Bible does not say how old Cain was when he killed Abel (Genesis 4:8). Since they were both farmers, they were likely both full-grown adults, possibly with families of their own. Adam and Eve surely had given birth to more children than just Cain and Abel at the time Abel was killed. They definitely had many more children later (Genesis 5:4). The fact that Cain was scared for his own life after he killed Abel (Genesis 4:14) indicates that there were likely many other children and perhaps even grandchildren of Adam and Eve already living at that time. Cain's wife (Genesis 4:17) was a daughter or granddaughter of Adam and Eve.

Since Adam and Eve were the first (and only) human beings, their children would have no other choice than to intermarry. God did not forbid inter-family marriage until much later when there were enough people to make intermarriage unnecessary (Leviticus 18:6-18). The reason that incest today often results in genetic abnormalities is that when two people of similar genetics (i.e., a brother and sister) have children together, there is a high risk of their recessive characteristics becoming dominant. When people from different families have children, it is highly unlikely that both parents will carry the same recessive traits. The human genetic code has become increasingly "polluted" over the centuries as genetic defects are multiplied, amplified, and passed down from generation to generation. Adam and Eve did not have any genetic defects, and that enabled them and the first few generations of their descendants to have a far greater quality of health than we do now. Adam and Eve's children had few, if any, genetic defects. As a result, it was safe for them to intermarry.

4. Question:
"What is the origin of the different races?"

Answer: The Bible does not explicitly give us the origin of the different "races" or skin colors in humanity. In actuality, there is only one race—the human race. Within the human race is diversity in skin color and other physical characteristics. Some speculate that when God confused the languages at the tower of Babel (Genesis 11:1-9), He also created racial diversity. It is possible that God made genetic changes to humanity to better enable people to survive in different ecologies, such as the darker skin of Africans being better equipped genetically to survive the excessive heat in Africa. According to this view, God confused the languages, causing humanity to segregate linguistically, and then created genetic racial differences based on where each racial group would eventually settle. While possible, there is no explicit biblical basis for this view. The races/skin colors of humanity are nowhere mentioned in connection with the tower of Babel.

After the flood, when the different languages came into existence, groups that spoke one language moved away with others of the same language. In doing so, the gene pool for a specific group shrank dramatically as the group no longer had the entire human population to mix with. Closer inbreeding took place, and in time certain features were emphasized in these different groups (all of which were present as a possibility in the genetic code). As further inbreeding occurred through the generations, the gene pool grew smaller and smaller, to the point that people of one language family all had the same or similar features.

Another explanation is that Adam and Eve possessed the genes to produce black, brown, and white offspring (and everything else in between). This would be similar to how a mixed-race couple sometimes has children that vary in color. Since God obviously desired humanity to be diverse in appearance, it makes sense that God would have given Adam and Eve the ability to produce children of different skin tones. Later, the only survivors of the flood were Noah and his wife, Noah's three sons and their wives—eight people in all (Genesis 7:13). Perhaps Noah's daughters-in-law were of different races. It is also possible that Noah's wife was of a different race than Noah. Maybe all eight of them were of mixed race, which would mean they possessed the genetics to produce children of different races. Whatever the explanation, the most important aspect of this question is that we are all the same race, all created by the same God, all created for the same purpose—to glorify Him.

5. Question:
"Why did the people in Genesis live such long lives?"

Answer: It is somewhat of a mystery why people in early chapters of Genesis lived such long lives. There are many theories put forward by biblical scholars. The genealogy in Genesis 5 records the line of the godly descendants of Adam—the line that would eventually produce the Messiah. God possibly blessed this line with especially long life as a result of their godliness and obedience. While this is a possible explanation, the Bible nowhere specifically limits the long lifespans to the individuals mentioned in Genesis chapter 5. Further, other than Enoch, Genesis 5 does not identify any of the individuals as being especially godly. It is likely that everyone at that time period lived several hundred years. Several factors probably contributed to this.

Genesis 1:6-7 mentions the water above the expanse, a canopy of water that surrounded the earth. Such a water canopy would have created a greenhouse effect and would have blocked much of the radiation that now hits the earth. This would have resulted in ideal living conditions. Genesis 7:11 indicates that, at the time of the flood, the water canopy was poured out on the earth, ending the ideal living conditions. Compare the life spans before the flood (Genesis 5:1-32) with those after the flood (Genesis 11:10-32). Immediately after the flood, the ages decreased dramatically.

Another consideration is that in the first few generations after creation, the human genetic code had developed few defects. Adam and Eve were created perfect. They were surely highly resistant to disease and illness. Their descendants would have inherited these advantages, albeit to lesser degrees. Over time, as a result of sin, the human genetic code became increasingly corrupted, and human beings became more and more susceptible to death and disease. This would also have resulted in drastically reduced lifespans.

6. Question:
"Why did God create us?"

Answer: The short answer to the question "why did God create us?" is "for His pleasure." Revelation 4:11 says, "You are worthy, our Lord and God, to receive glory and honor and power, for you created all things, and by your will they were created and have their being." Colossians 1:16 reiterates the point: "All things were created by him and for him." Being created for God's pleasure does not mean humanity was made to entertain God or provide Him with amusement. God is a creative Being, and it gives Him pleasure to create. God is a personal Being, and it gives Him pleasure to have other beings He can have a genuine relationship with.

Being made in the image and likeness of God (Genesis 1:27), human beings have the ability to know God and therefore love Him, worship Him, serve Him, and fellowship with Him. God did not create human beings because He needed them. As God, He needs nothing. In all eternity past, He felt no loneliness, so He was not looking for a "friend." He loves us, but this is not the same as needing us. If we had never existed, God would still be God—the unchanging One (Malachi 3:6). The I AM (Exodus 3:14) was never dissatisfied with His own eternal existence. When He made the universe, He did what pleased Himself, and since God is perfect, His action was perfect. "It was very good" (Genesis 1:31).

Also, God did not create "peers" or beings equal to Himself. Logically, He could not do so. If God were to create another being of equal power, intelligence, and perfection, then He would cease to be the one true God for the simple reason that there would be two gods—and that would be an impossibility. "The LORD is God; besides him there is no other" (Deuteronomy 4:35). Anything that God creates must of necessity be lesser than He. The thing made can never be greater than, or as great as, the One who made it.

Recognizing the complete sovereignty and holiness of God, we are amazed that He would take man and crown him "with glory and honor" (Psalm 8:5) and that He would condescend to call us "friends" (John 15:14-15). Why did God create us? God created us for His pleasure and so that we, as His creation, would have the pleasure of knowing Him.

7. Question:
"Can man live without God?"

Answer: Contrary to the claims of atheists and agnostics through the centuries, man cannot live without God. Man can have a mortal existence without acknowledging God, but not without the fact of God.

As the Creator, God originated human life. To say that man can exist apart from God is to say that a watch can exist without a watchmaker or a story can exist without a storyteller. We owe our being to the God in whose image we are made (Genesis 1:27). Our existence depends on God, whether we acknowledge His existence or not.
As the Sustainer, God continuously confers life (Psalm 104:10-32).

Hard Questions About Humanity

He is life (John 14:6), and all creation is held together by the power of Christ (Colossians 1:17). Even those who reject God receive their sustenance from Him: "He causes his sun to rise on the evil and the good, and sends rain on the righteous and the unrighteous" (Matthew 5:45). To think that man can live without God is to suppose a sunflower can continue to live without light or a rose without water.

As the Savior, God gives eternal life to those who believe. In Christ is life, which is the light of men (John 1:4). Jesus came that we may have life "and have it to the full" (John 10:10). All who place their trust in Him are promised eternity with Him (John 3:15-16). For man to live—truly live—he must know Christ (John 17:3).

Without God, man has physical life only. God warned Adam and Eve that on the day they rejected Him they would "surely die" (Genesis 2:17). As we know, they did disobey, but they did not die physically that day; rather, they died spiritually. Something inside them died—the spiritual life they had known, the communion with God, the freedom to enjoy Him, the innocence and purity of their soul—it was all gone.

Adam, who had been created to live and fellowship with God, was cursed with a completely carnal existence. What God had intended to go from dust to glory now was to go from dust to dust. Just like Adam, the man without God today still functions in an earthly existence. Such a person may seem to be happy; after all, there is enjoyment and pleasure to be had in this life. But even those enjoyments and pleasures cannot be fully received without a relationship with God.

Some who reject God live lives of diversion and merriment. Their fleshly pursuits seem to yield a carefree and gratified existence. The Bible says there is a certain measure of delight to be had in sin (Hebrews 11:25). The problem is that it is temporary; life in this world is short (Psalm 90:3-12). Sooner or later, the hedonist, like the prodigal son in the parable, finds that worldly pleasure is unsustainable (Luke 15:13-15).

Not everyone who rejects God is an empty pleasure-seeker, however. There are many unsaved people who live disciplined, sober lives—happy and fulfilled lives, even. The Bible presents certain moral principles which will benefit anyone in this world—fidelity, honesty, self-control, etc. But, again, without God man has only this world. Getting smoothly through this life is no guarantee that we are ready for the afterlife. See the parable of the rich farmer in Luke 12:16-21 and Jesus' exchange with the rich (but very moral) young man in Matthew 19:16-23.

Without God, man is unfulfilled, even in his mortal life. Man is not at peace with his fellow man because he is not at peace with himself. Man is restless with himself because he has no peace with God. The pursuit of pleasure for pleasure's sake is a sign of inner turmoil. Pleasure seekers throughout history have found over and over that the temporary diversions of life give way to a deeper despair. The nagging feeling that "something is wrong" is hard to shake off. King Solomon gave himself to a pursuit of all this world has to offer, and he recorded his findings in the book of Ecclesiastes.

Solomon discovered that knowledge, in and of itself, is futile (Ecclesiastes 1:12-18). He found that pleasure and wealth are futile (2:1-11), materialism is folly (2:12-23), and riches are fleeting (chapter 6).

Solomon concludes that life is God's gift (3:12-13) and the only wise way to live is to fear God: "Let us hear the conclusion of the whole matter: Fear God, and keep His commandments: for this is the whole duty of man. For God shall bring every work into judgment, with every secret thing, whether it be good, or whether it be evil" (12:13-14).

In other words, there is more to life than the physical dimension. Jesus stresses this point when He says, "Man does not live on bread alone, but on every word that comes from the mouth of God" (Matthew 4:4). Not bread (the physical) but God's Word (the spiritual) keeps us alive. It is useless for us to search within ourselves for the cure to all our miseries. Man can only find life and fulfillment when he acknowledges God.

Without God, man's destiny is hell. The man without God is spiritually dead; when his physical life is over, he faces eternal separation from God. In Jesus' narrative of the rich man and Lazarus (Luke 16:19-31), the rich man lives a pleasurable life of ease without a thought of God, while Lazarus suffers through his life but knows God. It is after their deaths that both men truly comprehend the gravity of the choices they made in life. The rich man realized, too late, that there is more to life than the pursuit of wealth. Meanwhile, Lazarus is comforted in paradise. For both men, the short duration of their earthly existence paled in comparison to the permanent state of their souls.

Man is a unique creation. God has set a sense of eternity in our hearts (Ecclesiastes 3:11), and that sense of timeless destiny can only find its fulfillment in God Himself.

8. Question:
"What does it mean that man is made in the image of God?"

Answer: On the last day of creation, God said, "Let us make man in our image, in our likeness" (Genesis 1:26). Thus, He finished His work with a "personal touch." God formed man from the dust and gave him life by sharing His own breath (Genesis 2:7). Accordingly, man is unique among all God's creations, having both a material body and an immaterial soul/spirit.

Having the "image" or "likeness" of God means, in the simplest terms, which we were made to resemble God. Adam did not resemble God in the sense of God's having flesh and blood. Scripture says that "God is spirit" (John 4:24) and therefore exists without a body. However, Adam's body did mirror the life of God insofar as it was created in perfect health and was not subject to death.

The image of God refers to the immaterial part of man. It sets man apart from the animal world, fits him for the dominion God intended him to have over the earth (Genesis 1:28), and enables him to commune with his Maker. It is a likeness mentally, morally, and socially.

Mentally, man was created as a rational, volitional agent. In other words, man can reason and man can choose. This is a reflection of God's intellect and freedom. Anytime someone invents a machine, writes a book, paints a landscape, enjoys a symphony, calculates a sum, or names a pet, he or she is proclaiming the fact that we are made in God's image.

Morally, man was created in righteousness and perfect innocence, a reflection of God's holiness. God saw all He had made (mankind included) and called it "very good" (Genesis 1:31). Our conscience or "moral compass" is a vestige of that original state. Whenever someone writes a law, recoils from evil, praises good behavior, or feels guilty, he is confirming the fact that we are made in God's own image.

Socially, man was created for fellowship. This reflects God's triune nature and His love. In Eden, man's primary relationship was with God (Genesis 3:8 implies fellowship with God), and God made the first woman because "it is not good for the man to be alone" (Genesis 2:18). Every time someone marries, makes a friend, hugs a child, or attends church, he is demonstrating the fact that we are made in the likeness of God.

Part of being made in God's image is that Adam had the capacity to make free choices. Although he was given a righteous nature, Adam made an evil choice to rebel against his Creator. In so doing, Adam marred the image of God within himself, and he passed that damaged likeness on to all his descendants (Romans 5:12). Today, we still bear the image of God (James 3:9), but we also bear the scars of sin. Mentally, morally, socially, and physically, we show the effects of sin. The good news is that when God redeems an individual, He begins to restore the original image of God, creating a "new self, created to be like God in true righteousness and holiness" (Ephesians 4:24). That redemption is only available by God's grace through faith in Jesus Christ as our Savior from the sin that separates us from God (Ephesians 2:8-9). Through Christ, we are made new creations in the likeness of God (2 Corinthians 5:17).

9. Question:
"Do we have two or three parts? Body, soul, and spirit? Dichotomy or trichotomy?"

Answer: Genesis 1:26-27 indicates that there is something that makes humanity distinct from all the other creations. Human beings were intended to have a relationship with God, and as such, God created us with both material and immaterial parts. The material is obviously that which is tangible: the physical body, bones, organs, etc., and exists as long as the person is alive. The immaterial aspects are those which are intangible: soul, spirit, intellect, will, conscience, etc. These exist beyond the physical lifespan of the individual.

All human beings possess both material and immaterial characteristics. It is clear that all mankind has a body containing flesh, blood, bones, organs, and cells. However, it is the intangible qualities of mankind that are often debated. What does Scripture say about these? Genesis 2:7 states that man was created as a living soul. Numbers 16:22 names God as the "God of the spirits" that are possessed by all mankind. Proverbs 4:23 tells us, "Above all else, guard your heart, for it is the wellspring of life," indicating that the heart is central to man's will and emotions. Acts 23:1 says, "Paul looked straight at the

Sanhedrin and said, 'My brothers, I have fulfilled my duty to God in all good conscience to this day.'" Here Paul refers to the conscience, that part of the mind that convicts us of right and wrong. Romans 12:2 states, "Do not conform any longer to the pattern of this world, but be transformed by the renewing of your mind." These verses, and numerous others, refer to the various aspects of the immaterial part of humanity. We all share both material and immaterial qualities.

So, Scripture outlines far more than just soul and spirit. Somehow, the soul, spirit, heart, conscience, and mind are connected and interrelated. The soul and spirit, though, definitely are the primary immaterial aspects of humanity. They likely comprise the other aspects. With this is mind, is humanity dichotomous (cut in two, body/soul-spirit), or trichotomous (cut in three, body/soul/spirit). It is impossible to be dogmatic. There are good arguments for both views. A key verse is Hebrews 4:12: "For the word of God is living and active. Sharper than any double-edged sword, it penetrates even to dividing soul and spirit, joints and marrow; it judges the thoughts and attitudes of the heart." This verse tells us at least two things about this debate. The soul and spirit can be divided, and the division of soul and spirit is something that only God can discern. Rather than focusing on something we cannot know for sure, it is better to focus on the Creator, who has made us "fearfully and wonderfully" (Psalm 139:14).

10. Question:
"What is the difference between the soul and spirit of man?"

Answer: The soul and the spirit are the two primary immaterial aspects that Scripture ascribes to humanity. It can be confusing to attempt to discern the precise differences between the two. The word "spirit" refers only to the immaterial facet of humanity. Human beings have a spirit, but are we not spirits. However, in Scripture, only

believers are said to be spiritually alive (1 Corinthians 2:11; Hebrews 4:12; James 2:26), while unbelievers are spiritually dead (Ephesians 2:1-5; Colossians 2:13). In Paul's writing, the spiritual was pivotal to the life of the believer (1 Corinthians 2:14; 3:1; Ephesians 1:3; 5:19; Colossians 1:9; 3:16). The spirit is the element in humanity which gives us the ability to have an intimate relationship with God.
Whenever the word "spirit" is used, it refers to the immaterial part of humanity that "connects" with God, who Himself is spirit (John 4:24).

The word "soul" can refer to both the immaterial and material aspects of humanity. Unlike human beings having a spirit, human beings are souls. In its most basic sense, the word "soul" means "life." However, beyond this essential meaning, the Bible speaks of the soul in many contexts. One of these is humanity's eagerness to sin (Luke 12:26). Humanity is naturally evil, and our souls are tainted as a result. The life principle of the soul is removed at the time of physical death (Genesis 35:18; Jeremiah 15:2). The soul, as with the spirit, is the center of many spiritual and emotional experiences (Job 30:25; Psalm 43:5; Jeremiah 13:17). Whenever the word "soul" is used, it can refer to the whole person, whether alive or in the afterlife.

The soul and the spirit are connected, but separable (Hebrews 4:12). The soul is the essence of humanity's being; it is who we are. The spirit is the aspect of humanity that connects with God.

11. Question:
"How are human souls created?"

Answer: There are two biblically plausible views on how the human soul is created. Traducianism is the theory that a soul is generated by the physical parents along with the physical body. Support for Traducianism is as follows: (A) In Genesis 2:7, God breathed the breath of life into Adam, causing Adam to become a "living soul."

Scripture nowhere records God performing this action again. (B) Adam had a son in his own likeness (Genesis 5:3). Adam's descendants seem to be "living souls" without God breathing into them. (C) Genesis 2:2-3 seems to indicate that God ceased His creative work. (D) Adam's sin affects all men—both physically and spiritually—this makes sense if the body and soul both come from the parents. The weakness of Traducianism is that it is unclear how an immaterial soul can be generated through an entirely physical process. Traducianism can only be true if the body and soul are inextricably connected.

Creationism is the view that God creates a new soul when a human being is conceived. Creationism was held by many early church fathers and also has scriptural support. First, Scripture differentiates the origin of the soul from the origin of the body (Ecclesiastes 12:7; Isaiah 42:5; Zechariah 12:1; Hebrews 12:9). Second, if God creates each individual soul at the moment it is needed, the separation of soul and body is held firm. The weakness of Creationism is that it has God continually creating new human souls, while Genesis 2:2-3 indicates that God ceased creating. Also, since the entire human existence— body, soul, and spirit—are infected by sin and God creates a new soul for every human being, how is that soul then infected with sin?

A third view, but one that lacks biblical support, is the concept that God created all human souls at the same time, and "attaches" a soul to a human being at the moment of conception. This view holds that there is sort of a "warehouse of souls" in heaven where God stores souls that await a human body to be attached to. Again, this view has no biblical support, and is usually held by those of a "new age" or reincarnation mindset.

Whether the Traducianist view or the Creationist view is correct, both agree that the soul does not exist prior to conception. This seems to be the clear teaching of the Bible. Whether God creates a new human soul at the moment of conception, or whether God designed the human reproductive process to also reproduce a soul, God is ultimately responsible for the creation of each and every human soul.

12. Question:
"Is the human soul mortal or immortal?"

Answer: Without a doubt the human soul is immortal. This is clearly seen in many Scriptures in both the Old and New Testaments: Psalm 22:26; 23:6; 49:7-9; Ecclesiastes 12:7; Daniel 12:2-3; Matthew 25:46; and 1 Corinthians 15:12-19. Daniel 12:2 says, "Multitudes who sleep in the dust of the earth will awake: some to everlasting life, others to shame and everlasting contempt." Similarly, Jesus Himself said that the wicked "will go away to eternal punishment, but the righteous to eternal life" (Matthew 25:46). With the same Greek word used to refer to both "punishment" and "life," it is clear that both the wicked and the righteous have an eternal/immortal soul.

The unmistakable teaching of the Bible is that all people, whether they are saved or lost, will exist eternally, in either heaven or hell. True life or spiritual life does not cease when our fleshly bodies pass away in death. Our souls will live forever, either in the presence of God in heaven if we are saved, or in punishment in hell if we reject God's gift of salvation. In fact, the promise of the Bible is that not only will our souls live forever, but also that our bodies will be resurrected. This hope of a bodily resurrection is at the very heart of the Christian faith (1 Corinthians 15:12-19).

While all souls are immortal, it is important to remember that we are not eternal in the same way that God is. God is the only truly eternal being in that He alone is without a beginning or end. God has always existed and will always continue to exist. All other sentient creatures, whether they are human or angelic, are finite in that they had a beginning. While our souls will live forever once we come into being, the Bible does not support the concept that our souls have always existed. Our souls are immortal, as that is how God created them, but they did have a beginning; there was a time they did not exist.

13. Question:
"Does everyone have a "God-shaped hole?"

Answer: The "God-shaped hole" concept states that every person has a void in his soul/spirit/life that can only be filled by God. The "God-shaped hole" is the innate longing of the human heart for something outside itself, something transcendent, something "other." Ecclesiastes 3:11 refers to God's placing of "eternity in man's heart." God made humanity for His eternal purpose, and only God can fulfill our desire for eternity. All religion is based on the innate desire to "connect" with God. This desire can only be fulfilled by God, and therefore can be likened to a "God-shaped hole."

The problem, though, is that humanity ignores this hole or attempts to fill it with things other than God. Jeremiah 17:9 describes the condition of our hearts: "The heart is deceitful above all things and beyond cure. Who can understand it?" Solomon reiterates the same concept: "The hearts of men, moreover, are full of evil and there is madness in their hearts while they live…" (Ecclesiastes 9:3). The New Testament concurs: "The sinful mind is hostile to God. It does not submit to God's law, nor can it do so" (Romans 8:7). Romans 1:18-22 describes humanity ignoring what can be known about God, including presumably the "God-shaped hole," and instead worshipping anything and everything other than God.

Sadly, too many spend their lives looking for something other than God to fill their longing for meaning—business, family, sports, etc. But in pursuing these things that are not eternal, they remain unfulfilled and wonder why their lives never seem satisfactory. There is no doubt that many people pursuing things other than God achieve a measure of "happiness" for a time. But when we consider Solomon, who had all the riches, success, esteem, and power in the world—in short, all that men seek after in this life—we see that none of it fulfilled the longing for eternity. He declared it all "vanity," meaning that he sought after these things in vain because they did not satisfy. In the end he said, "Now all has been heard; here is the conclusion of the matter: Fear God and keep his commandments, for this is the whole [duty] of man" (Ecclesiastes 12:13).

Just as a square peg cannot fill a round hole, neither can the "God-shaped hole" inside each of us be filled by anyone or anything other than God. Only through a personal relationship with God through faith in Jesus Christ can the "God-shaped hole" be filled and the desire for eternity fulfilled.

14. Question:
"What does the Bible say about cremation? Is it wrong to cremate a person's body?"

Answer: The Bible does not give any specific teaching about cremation. There are occurrences in the Old Testament of people being burned to death (1 Kings 16:18; 2 Kings 21:6) and of human bones being burned (2 Kings 23:16-20), but these are not examples of cremation. It is interesting to note that in 2 Kings 23:16-20, burning human bones on an altar desecrated the altar. At the same time, the Old Testament law nowhere commands that a deceased human body not be burned, nor does it attach any curse or judgment on someone who is cremated.

Cremation was practiced in biblical times, but it was not commonly practiced by the Israelites or by New Testament believers. In the cultures of Bible times, burial in a tomb, cave, or in the ground was the common way to dispose of a human body (Genesis 23:19; 35:4; 2 Chronicles 16:14; Matthew 27:60-66). While burial was the common practice, the Bible nowhere commands burial as the only allowed method of disposing of a body.

Is cremation something a Christian can consider? Again, there is no explicit scriptural command against cremation. Some believers object to the practice of cremation on the basis it does not recognize that one day God will resurrect our bodies and re-unite them with our soul/spirit (1 Corinthians 15:35-58; 1 Thessalonians 4:16). However, the fact that a body has been cremated does not make it any more difficult for God to resurrect that body. The bodies of Christians who died a thousand years ago have, by now, completely turned into dust. This will in no way prevent God from being able to resurrect their bodies. He created them in the first place; He will have no difficulty re-creating them. Cremation does nothing but "expedite" the process of turning a body into dust. God is equally able to raise a person's remains that have been cremated as He is the remains of a person who was not cremated. The question of burial or cremation is within the realm of Christian freedom. A person or a family considering this issue should pray for wisdom (James 1:5) and follow the conviction that results.

15. Question:
"What is the Christian view of human cloning?"

Answer: While the Bible does not specifically deal with the subject of human cloning, there are principles in Scripture which may shed more light on the concept. Cloning requires both DNA and embryo cells. First, DNA is removed from the nucleus of a creature's cell. The material, bearing coded genetic information, is then placed in the nucleus of an embryonic cell. The cell receiving the new genetic information would have had its own DNA removed in order to accept the new DNA. If the cell accepts the new DNA, a duplicate embryo is formed. However, the embryo cell may reject the new DNA and die. Also, it is very possible that the embryo may not survive having the original genetic material removed from its nucleus. In many cases, when cloning is attempted, several embryos are used in order to increase the odds of a successful implantation of new genetic material. While it is possible for a duplicate creature to be created in this manner (for example, Dolly the sheep), the chances of successfully duplicating a creature without variations, and without complication, are extremely slim.

The Christian view of the process of human cloning can be stated in light of several scriptural principles. First, human beings are created in the image of God and, therefore, are unique. Genesis 1:26-27 asserts that man is created in God's image and likeness and is unique among all creations. Clearly, human life is something to be valued and not treated like a commodity to be bought and sold. Some people have promoted human cloning for the purpose of creating replacement organs for people in need of transplants who cannot find a suitable donor. The thinking is that to take one's own DNA and create a duplicate organ composed of that DNA would greatly reduce the chances of organ rejection. While this may be true, the problem is that doing so cheapens human life. The process of cloning requires human embryos to be used. While cells can be generated to make new organs, it is necessary to kill several embryos to obtain the required DNA. In essence the cloning would "throw away" many human embryos as "waste material," eliminating the chance for those embryos to grow into full maturity.

Many people believe that life does not begin at conception with the formation of the embryo, and therefore embryos are not really human beings. The Bible teaches differently. Psalm 139:13-16 says, "For you created my inmost being; you knit me together in my mother's womb. I praise you because I am fearfully and wonderfully made; your works are wonderful, I know that full well. My frame was not hidden from you when I was made in the secret place. When I was woven together in the depths of the earth, your eyes saw my unformed body. All the days ordained for me were written in your book before one of them came to be." The writer, David, declares that he was known personally by God before he was born, meaning that at his conception he was a human being with a God-ordained future.

Further, Isaiah 49:1-5 speaks of God calling Isaiah to his ministry as a prophet while he was still in his mother's womb. Also, John the Baptist was filled with the Holy Spirit while he was still in the womb (Luke 1:15). All of this points to the Bible's stand on life beginning at conception. In light of this, human cloning, with its destruction of human embryos, would not be consistent with the Bible's view of human life.

In addition, if humanity was created, then there must be a Creator, and humanity is therefore subject and accountable to that Creator. Although popular thinking—secular psychology and humanistic thought—would have one believe that man is accountable to no one but himself and that man is the ultimate authority, the Bible teaches differently. God created man and gave him responsibility over the earth (Genesis 1:28-29, 9:1-2). With this responsibility comes accountability to God. Man is not the ultimate authority over himself, and he is therefore not in a position to make decisions about the value of human life. Neither, then, is science the authority by which the ethics of human cloning, abortion, or euthanasia are decided. According to the Bible, God is the only one who rightfully exercises sovereign control over human life. To attempt to control such things is to place oneself in God's position. Clearly, man is not to do this.

If we view man as simply another creature and not as the unique creation he is, it is not difficult to see human beings as mere mechanisms needing maintenance and repair. But we are not just a collection of molecules and chemicals. The Bible teaches that God created each of us and has a specific plan for each of us. Further,

He seeks a personal relationship with each of us through His Son, Jesus Christ. While there are aspects of human cloning which may seem beneficial, mankind has no control over where cloning technology may go. It is foolish to assume that only good intentions will direct the utilization of cloning. Man is not in a position to exercise the responsibility or judgment that would be required to govern the cloning of human beings.

A frequent question is whether a cloned human being, assuming that human cloning is one day successful, would have a soul. Genesis 2:7 says, "And the LORD God formed man of the dust of the ground, and breathed into his nostrils the breath of life; and man became a living soul." Here is the description of God creating a living, human soul. Souls are what we are, not what we have (1 Corinthians 15:45). The question is what kind of living soul would be created by human cloning? That is not a question that can be conclusively answered. It seems, though, that if a human being were successfully cloned, the clone would be just as much of a human being, including having an eternal soul, as any other human being.

16. Question:
"What does the Bible say about racism, prejudice, and discrimination?"

Answer: The first thing to understand in this discussion is that there is only one race—the human race. Caucasians, Africans, Asians, Indians, Arabs, and Jews are not different races. Rather, they are different ethnicities of the human race. All human beings have the same physical characteristics (with minor variations, of course). More importantly, all human beings are created in the image and likeness of God (Genesis 1:26-27). God loved the world so much that He sent Jesus to lay down His life for us (John 3:16). The "world" obviously includes all ethnic groups.

God does not show partiality or favoritism (Deuteronomy 10:17; Acts 10:34; Romans 2:11; Ephesians 6:9), and neither should we. James 2:4 describes those who discriminate as "judges with evil thoughts." Instead, we are to love our neighbors as ourselves (James 2:8). In the Old Testament, God divided humanity into two "racial" groups: Jews and Gentiles. God's intent was for the Jews to be a kingdom of priests, ministering to the Gentile nations. Instead, for the most part, the Jews became proud of their status and despised the Gentiles. Jesus Christ put an end to this, destroying the dividing wall of hostility (Ephesians 2:14). All forms of racism, prejudice, and discrimination are affronts to the work of Christ on the cross.

Jesus commands us to love one another as He loves us (John 13:34). If God is impartial and loves us with impartiality, then we need to love others with that same high standard. Jesus teaches in Matthew 25 that whatever we do to the least of His brothers, we do to Him. If we treat a person with contempt, we are mistreating a person created in God's image; we are hurting somebody whom God loves and for whom Jesus died.

Racism, in varying forms and to various degrees, has been a plague on humanity for thousands of years. Brothers and sisters of all ethnicities, this should not be. Victims of racism, prejudice, and discrimination need to forgive. Ephesians 4:32 declares, "Be kind and compassionate to one another, forgiving each other, just as in Christ God forgave you." Racists may not deserve your forgiveness, but we deserved God's forgiveness far less. Those who practice racism, prejudice, and discrimination need to repent. "Present yourselves to God as being alive from the dead, and your members as instruments of righteousness to God" (Romans 6:13). May Galatians 3:28 be completely realized, "There is neither Jew nor Greek, slave nor free, male nor female, for you are all one in Christ Jesus."

17. Question:
"What does the Bible say about the death penalty / capital punishment?"

Answer: The Old Testament law commanded the death penalty for various acts: murder (Exodus 21:12), kidnapping (Exodus 21:16), bestiality (Exodus 22:19), adultery (Leviticus 20:10), homosexuality (Leviticus 20:13), being a false prophet (Deuteronomy 13:5), prostitution and rape (Deuteronomy 22:24), and several other crimes. However, God often showed mercy when the death penalty was due. David committed adultery and murder, yet God did not demand his life be taken (2 Samuel 11:1-5, 14-17; 2 Samuel 12:13). Ultimately, every sin we commit should result in the death penalty because the wages of sin is death (Romans 6:23). Thankfully, God demonstrates His love for us in not condemning us (Romans 5:8).

When the Pharisees brought a woman who was caught in the act of adultery to Jesus and asked Him if she should be stoned, Jesus replied, "If any one of you is without sin, let him be the first to throw a stone at her" (John 8:7). This should not be used to indicate that Jesus rejected capital punishment in all instances. Jesus was simply exposing the hypocrisy of the Pharisees. The Pharisees wanted to trick Jesus into breaking the Old Testament law; they did not truly care about the woman being stoned (where was the man who was caught in adultery?) God is the One who instituted capital punishment: "Whoever sheds man's blood, by man his blood shall be shed, for in the image of God He made man" (Genesis 9:6). Jesus would support capital punishment in some instances. Jesus also demonstrated grace when capital punishment was due (John 8:1-11). The apostle Paul definitely recognized the power of the government to institute capital punishment where appropriate (Romans 13:1-7).

How should a Christian view the death penalty? First, we must remember that God has instituted capital punishment in His Word; therefore, it would be presumptuous of us to think that we could institute a higher standard. God has the highest standard of any being; He is perfect. This standard applies not only to us but to Himself. Therefore, He loves to an infinite degree, and He has mercy to an infinite degree. We also see that He has wrath to an infinite degree, and it is all maintained in a perfect balance.

Second, we must recognize that God has given government the authority to determine when capital punishment is due (Genesis 9:6; Romans 13:1-7). It is unbiblical to claim that God opposes the death penalty in all instances. Christians should never rejoice when the death penalty is employed, but at the same time, Christians should not fight against the government's right to execute the perpetrators of the most evil of crimes.

18. Question:
"What does the Bible say about euthanasia and/or having a living will?"

Answer: Euthanasia can be a very difficult issue. There are two sides that are difficult to balance. On one end, we do not want to take a person's life into our own hands and end it prematurely. On the other end, at what point do we simply allow a person to die and take no further action to preserve life?

The overriding truth that drives the conclusion that God is opposed to euthanasia is His sovereignty. We know that physical death is inevitable (Psalm 89:48; Hebrews 9:27). However, God alone is sovereign over when and how a person's death occurs. Job testifies in Job 30:23, "I know you will bring me down to death, to the place appointed for all the living." Ecclesiastes 8:8a declares, "No man has power over the wind to contain it; so no one has power over the day of his death." God has the final say over death (see also 1 Corinthians 15:26, 54-56; Hebrews 2:9, 14-15; Revelation 21:4). Euthanasia is man's way of trying to usurp that authority from God.

Death is a natural occurrence. Sometimes God allows a person to suffer for a long time before death occurs; other times, the person's suffering is cut short. No one enjoys suffering, but that does not make it right to determine that a person is ready to die. Often God's purposes are made known through a person's suffering. "When times are good, be happy; but when times are bad, consider: God has made the one as well as the other…" (Ecclesiastes 7:14). Romans 5:3 teaches that tribulations bring about perseverance. God cares about those who are crying out for death to end their suffering. God gives purpose to life even to the end. Only God knows what is best, and His timing, even in the matter of one's death, is perfect.

At the same time, the Bible does not command us to do everything we can to keep a person alive. If a person is being kept alive only by machines, it is not immoral to turn off the machines and allow the person to die. If a person has been in a persistent vegetative state for a prolonged period of time, it would not be an offense to God to remove whatever tubes/machines that are keeping the person's body alive. Should God desire to keep a person alive, He is perfectly capable of doing so without the help of feeding tubes and/or machines.

Making a decision like this one is very difficult and painful. It is never easy to tell a doctor to end the life support of a loved one. We should never seek to prematurely end a life, but at the same time, neither do we have to go to extraordinary means to preserve a life. The best advice to anyone facing this decision is to pray to God for wisdom (James 1:5).

19. Question:
"Is there an age limit to how long we can live?"

Answer: Many people understand Genesis 6:3 to be a 120-year age limit on humanity, "Then the LORD said, 'My Spirit will not contend with man forever, for he is mortal; his days will be a hundred and twenty years.'" However, Genesis chapter 11 records several people living past the age of 120. As a result, some interpret Genesis 6:3 to mean that, as a general rule, people will no longer live past 120 years of age. After the flood, the life spans began to shrink dramatically (compare Genesis 5 with Genesis 11) and eventually shrank to below 120 (Genesis 11:24). Since that time, very few people have lived past 120 years old.

However, another interpretation, which seems to be more in keeping with the context, is that Genesis 6:3 is God's declaration that the flood would occur 120 years from His pronouncement. Humanity's days being ended is a reference to humanity itself being destroyed in the flood. Some dispute this interpretation due to the fact that God commanded Noah to build the ark when Noah was 500 years old in Genesis 5:32 and Noah was 600 years old when the flood came (Genesis 7:6); only giving 100 years of time, not 120 years. However, the timing of God's pronouncement of Genesis 6:3 is not given. Further, Genesis 5:32 is not the time that God commanded Noah to build the Ark, but rather the age Noah was when he became the father of his three sons. It is perfectly plausible that God determined the flood to occur in 120 years and then waited several years before He commanded Noah to build the ark. Whatever the case, the 100 years between Genesis 5:32 and 7:6 in no way contradicts the 120 years mentioned in Genesis 6:3.

Several hundred years after the flood, Moses declared, "The length of our days is seventy years—or eighty, if we have the strength; yet their span is but trouble and sorrow, for they quickly pass, and we fly away" (Psalm 90:10). Neither Genesis 6:3 nor Psalm 90:10 are God-ordained age limits for humanity. Genesis 6:3 is a prediction of the timetable for the flood. Psalm 90:10 is simply stating that as a general rule, people live 70-80 years (which is still true today).

20. Question:
"Are we all God's children, or only Christians?"

Answer: The Bible is clear that all people are God's creation (Colossians 1:16), and that God loves the entire world (John 3:16), but only those who are born again are children of God (John 1:12; 11:52; Romans 8:16; 1 John 3:1-10).

In Scripture, the lost are never referred to as children of God. Ephesians 2:3 tells us that before we were saved we were "by nature objects of wrath." Romans 9:8 says that "it is not the natural children who are God's children, but it is the children of the promise who are regarded as Abraham's offspring." Instead of being born as God's children, we are born in sin, which separates us from God and aligns us with Satan as God's enemy (James 4:4; 1 John 3:8). Jesus said, "If God were your Father, you would love me, for I came from God and now am here. I have not come on my own; but he sent me" (John 8:42). Then a few verses later in John 8:44, Jesus told the Pharisees that they "belong to your father, the devil, and you want to carry out your father's desire." The fact that those who are not saved are not children of God is also seen in 1 John 3:10: "This is how we know who the children of God are and who the children of the devil are: Anyone who does not do what is right is not a child of God; nor is anyone who does not love his brother."

We become children of God when we are saved because we are adopted into God's family through our relationship with Jesus Christ (Galatians 4:5-6; Ephesians 1:5). This can be clearly seen in verses like Romans 8:14-17: "...because those who are led by the Spirit of God are sons of God. For you did not receive a spirit that makes you a slave again to fear, but you received the Spirit of son-ship. And by him we cry, 'Abba, Father.' The Spirit himself testifies with our spirit that we are God's children. Now if we are children, then we are heirs—heirs of God and co-heirs with Christ, if indeed we share in his sufferings in order that we may also share in his glory." Those who are saved are children "of God through faith in Christ Jesus" (Galatians 3:26) because God has "predestined us to be adopted as his sons through Jesus Christ, in accordance with his pleasure and will" (Ephesians 1:5).

21. Question:
"What does it mean that we are fearfully and wonderfully made (Psalm 139:14)?"

Answer: Psalm 139:14 declares, "I praise you because I am fearfully and wonderfully made; your works are wonderful, I know that full well." The context of this verse is the incredible nature of our physical bodies. The human body is the most complex and unique organism in the world, and that complexity and uniqueness speaks volumes about the mind of its Creator. Every aspect of the body, down to the tiniest microscopic cell, reveals that it is fearfully and wonderfully made.

Engineers understand how to design strong yet light beams by putting the strong material toward the outside edges of a cross-section and filling the inside with lighter, weaker material. This is done because the greatest amounts of stress occur on the surfaces of a structure when handling common bending or stresses. A cross section of a human bone reveals that the strong material is on the outside and the inside is used as a factory for blood cells of various kinds. When you examine a sophisticated camera with its ability to let in more or less light as needed and its ability to focus automatically over a vast range of field, you find repeated imitations of the operation of the human eye. Yet, having two eyeballs, we also have depth perception which gives us the ability to judge how far away an object is.

The human brain is also an amazing organ, fearfully and wonderfully made. It has the ability to learn, reason, and control so many automatic functions of the body such as heart rate, blood pressure, and breathing, and to maintain balance to walk, run, stand, and sit, all while concentrating on something else. Computers can outdo the human brain in raw calculating power but are primitive when it comes to performing most reasoning tasks. The brain also has an amazing ability to adapt. In an experiment, when people put on glasses that made the world seem upside down, their brains quickly reinterpreted the information they were being given to perceive the world as "right-side-up." When others were blindfolded for long periods of time, the "vision center" of the brain soon began to be used for other functions. When people move to a house near a railroad, soon the sound of the trains is filtered out by their brains, and they lose conscious thought of the noise.

When it comes to miniaturization, the human body is also a marvel fearfully and wonderfully made. For instance, information needed for the replication of an entire human body, with every detail covered, is stored in the double-helix DNA strand found in the nucleus of each of the billions of cells in the human body. And the system of information and control represented by our nervous system is amazingly compact in comparison to man's clumsy inventions of wires and optical cables. Each cell, once called a "simple" cell, is a tiny factory not yet fully understood by man. As microscopes become more and more powerful, the incredible vistas of the human cell begin to come into focus.

Consider the single fertilized cell of a newly conceived human life. From that one cell within the womb develop all the different kinds of tissues, organs, and systems, all working together at just the right time in an amazingly coordinated process. An example is the hole in the septum between the two ventricles in the heart of the newborn infant. This hole closes up at exactly the right time during the birth process to allow for the oxygenation of the blood from the lungs, which does not occur while the baby is in the womb and is receiving oxygen through the umbilical cord.

Further, the body's immune system is able to fight off so many enemies and restore itself from the smallest repair (even repairing bad portions of DNA) to the largest (mending bones and recovering from major accidents). Yes, there are diseases that will eventually overcome the body as we age, but we have no idea how many times through a lifetime that our immune systems have saved us from certain death.

The functions of the human body are also incredible. The ability to handle large, heavy objects and to also carefully manipulate a delicate object without breaking it is also amazing. We can shoot a bow with the arrow repeatedly hitting a distant target, peck away quickly at a computer keyboard without thinking about the keys, crawl, walk, run, twirl around, climb, swim, do somersaults and flips, and perform "simple" tasks such as unscrewing a light bulb, brushing our teeth, and lacing up our shoes—again without thinking. Indeed, these are "simple" things, but man has yet to design and program a robot that is able to perform such a vast range of tasks and motions.

The function of the digestive tract and the related organs, the longevity of the heart, the formation and function of nerves and of blood vessels, the cleansing of the blood through the kidneys, the complexity of the inner and middle ear, the sense of taste and smell, and so many other things we barely understand—each one is a marvel and beyond man's ability to duplicate. Truly, we are fearfully and wonderfully made. How grateful we are to know the Creator—through His Son, Jesus Christ—and to marvel not only at

His knowledge but also at His love (Psalm 139:17-24).

22. Question:
"How should a Christian view genetic engineering?"

Answer: Because genetic engineering was unknown at the time that the Bible was written, it is difficult to establish definitive references on that topic alone. In order to determine the Christian view of genetic engineering, we need to establish a grid of principles through which to view genetic engineering. For specifics on the Christian view of cloning please see "What is the Christian view of cloning?"

The element of greatest concern about the issue of genetic engineering involves how much liberty mankind can take in its responsibility to care for the human body and the rest of creation. There is no doubt that the Bible exhorts us to be responsible for our physical health. Proverbs refers to certain activities regarding restoring the health of an individual (Proverbs 12:18). The Apostle Paul states that we have a certain duty to care for the body (Ephesians 5:29). He also encouraged his protégé, Timothy, to take medicinal action for his infirmities (1 Timothy 5:23). We are also aware that believers have the distinct responsibility of responding properly with the body in that it is the temple of the Holy Spirit (1 Corinthians 6:19,20). We are to show our faith by offering assistance to those who have physical needs (James 2:16). Therefore, we can conclude that as Christians we should be concerned about physical well-being and the benefits of securing help with our health.

Second, the creation was to be under the care of humans (Genesis 1:28; 2:15-20), but the Bible tells us that creation was impacted by the sin of humans (Genesis 3:17-19, Romans 8:19-21) and anticipates being redeemed from its effects. It is possible to conclude that as caretakers for the creation, humans have an obligation to

33

"fix" the effects of the sin curse and attempt to bring things into a better alignment, using any means possible. Therefore, the thinking goes, scientific advances could be used for the betterment of the creation. However, there are concerns regarding employing genetic engineering to accomplish this good.

1. There is the concern that genetic engineering will take on a role beyond what God has given to us as His creation. The Bible states that all things were created by God and for Him (Colossians 1:16). As individuals we are made in God's image and therefore should be subject to His plan (Genesis 1:26,27; Matthew 22:20,21). God designed all living things after certain "kinds" (Genesis 1:11-25). Too much manipulation of the genetics (altering species) could be delving into issues reserved for the Designer.

2. There is the concern of genetic engineering attempting to preclude God's plan for the restoration of creation. As stated above, the creation was affected by the events recorded in Genesis 3 (mankind's rebellion against God's plan). Death entered into the world, and man's genetic make-up and that of the rest of creation began a change toward demise. In some instances, genetic engineering could be seen as an attempt to undo this result called the "curse." However, God has said that He has a remedy for this—redemption through Jesus Christ, as described in Romans 8 and 1 Corinthians 15. The creation anticipates newness associated with the culmination of God's promise to restore things to an even better state than the original. To go "too far" to fight this process may compete with the responsibility of individuals to trust in Christ for restoration (Philippians 3:21).

3. It seems evident from general scriptural study that God has a plan for the process of life. It seems evident that the process is unique and purposeful. There is concern that if humanity interferes with that process, something could go terribly wrong. For example, Psalm 139 describes an intimate relationship between the psalmist and his Creator from the womb. Would the use of genetic manipulation to create life outside of God's plan jeopardize the development of a God-conscious soul? Would interfering with the process of physical life affect the prospects of spiritual life? Romans 5:12 tells us that all humanity sins because Adam sinned. It is understood that this involved the transference of the sin nature from generation to generation so that all have sinned (Romans 3:23). Paul explains the hope of eternity through the conquering of Adam's sin. If all that are in Adam (from his seed) die, and Christ died for those in such condition, could life created outside of that "seed" be redeemed? (1 Corinthians 15:22, 23).

4. There is also the concern that such bold strides in genetic engineering are motivated by a defiance of God. Genesis 11:1-9 discusses what happens when the creation attempts to exalt itself above the Creator. The people in Genesis 11 were unified, yet they were not submissive to God's design. As a result, God stopped their progress. God certainly recognized that there were some dangers involved with the direction in which the people were headed. We have a similar warning in Romans 1:18-32. There God describes individuals that have become so enamored with the creation (actually worshipping it rather than the Creator) that those individuals spiraled down to destruction. There is a danger that genetic engineering could foster similar motivations, and ultimately, similar results.

These are questions and issues for which we have no answers at present, but they are concerns, which should be carefully considered by Christians attempting to adopt a view of genetic engineering.

23. Question:
"What is the Table of Nations?"

Answer: Genesis chapter 10, commonly known as the Table of Nations, is a list of the patriarchal founders of seventy nations which descended from Noah through his three sons, Shem, Ham and Japheth. Twenty-six of the seventy descended from Shem, thirty from Ham and fourteen from Japheth. The 32nd verse sums up the chapter succinctly: "These are the families of the sons of Noah, according to their genealogies, by their nations; and out of these the nations were separated on the earth after the flood." Chapter 11 recounts their division at Babel.

The text seems to imply, though it never explicitly states, that the list was intended to be an exhaustive account. It has traditionally been interpreted as such. Nevertheless, this interpretation is speculative.

All of the Biblical genealogies are abridged. Key historical figures are included while "lesser," or less culturally relevant, siblings are left out. It is possible that such is the case for the Table of Nations. The compiler of the Table may have focused his ethnology on the nations most significant to his own nation at the time of the Table's compilation, while neglecting the founders of other far-flung, perhaps even long-forgotten nations. While every nation is ultimately related to every other nation through Noah, this ancestral tie does not indefinitely perpetuate mutual cultural significance among his descendants. As the old adage goes, "Out of sight, out of mind."

While some of the nations listed are easily identifiable, some remain obscure. Numerous scholars have attempted to identify these unknown nations with varying degrees of success. Due to the archaic nature of the source material, there remains considerable ambiguity.

The accuracy of the Table has been called into question by the fact that some of the relationships described do not match up with modern comparative linguistics. For example, the Elamites are said to have descended from Shem, yet their language was not Semitic. The Canaanites are said to have descended from Ham, yet their language was Semitic.

This objection assumes that these languages never experienced any dramatic change. The region's history seems to suggest that this is a dubious assumption. The cultures of the region were constantly subject to migrations and invasions by foreign powers. The conquering empires often imposed their language and culture upon the vanquished.

The Hellenizing of the Persian Empire following Alexander the Great's conquest is a classic example. Or consider the Israelites, who primarily spoke ancient Hebrew up until the Babylonian captivity and the Persian conquest. Then they adopted Aramaic, the official language of the Persian Empire. The Jewish Talmud was written in Aramaic, as were large portions of the books of Daniel and Ezra. Aramaic is thought to have been Jesus' native language. Following Alexander's conquest of Persia, the Jews adopted Greek as a second language. As a result, all of the New Testament was written in Greek. The languages of the region were not static.

The Hebrews invaded and conquered Canaan long before the Greeks, Persians and Babylonians. Is it any wonder that the Canaanites of the region adopted a Semitic language almost identical to ancient Hebrew? As for the Elamites, if we want to make a case from Elamite we have to start with proto-Elamite. Proto-Elamite remains un-deciphered, so it cannot form the basis for a polemic against the Table of Nations. There is no evidence that the later, non-Semitic Elamite underlies proto-Elamite, and we do not know what influences may have altered the language at any time.

Another objection to the Table of Nations is that several of the nations listed do not appear in the historical record (as we have it today) until as late as the first millennium B.C. This has led some critical scholars to date the Table no earlier than 7th century B.C.

This is a recurring criticism of the Bible. Rather than give the Bible the benefit of the doubt whenever it mentions a city or culture that doesn't appear anywhere else in the historical record, or whenever it places a culture in an era that antedates any other record we have from our other limited sources, critics generally assume that the biblical authors were either disingenuous or ignorant. Such was the case for the ancient metropolis of Nineveh and the ancient Hittite civilization of the Levant, both of which were rediscovered in modern times, in the 19th and 20th centuries, respectively, in a remarkable vindication of the Bible's historical witness. The fact of the matter is our knowledge of ancient cultures is extremely fragmented and often dependent upon key assumptions. It is therefore speculative to argue that the Table of Nations was written so late based solely on the fact that some of the nations mentioned appear nowhere else than in later historical records.

One final objection concerns the fact that Nimrod is said to have been a son of Cush (10:8), who is believed to have founded Nubia just south of Egypt. Yet Nimrod established several cities in Mesopotamia that show no sign of Nubian origin (10:8-12). Does this mean, as some critics claim, that the Table is therefore manifestly wrong, either about Nimrod's lineage or his role in establishing the Mesopotamian cities?

Skeptics who make this argument overlook the fact that Cush also fathered the founders of at least six Arabian nations (10:7), none of which show signs of Nubian origin. This is because Nubia developed along its own cultural path over many generations. Nimrod was an immediate son of Cush. We have no reason to expect him or the cities he helped establish to show any sign of Nubian origin.

In summary, the Table of Nations presents the biblical, ethnological view that all nations descend from Noah through three of his sons, Shem, Ham and Japheth. It is not known whether the list of seventy was meant to be exhaustive or if there were some nations left out, intentionally or accidentally. The accuracy of what we do know about the Table has been called into question by skeptics whose polemical objections tend to be defective and insubstantial. Due to the archaic nature of the source material, the veracity of the Table ultimately remains undeterminable. In the end, those who accept it do so by faith, taking it for granted as part of a larger, justifiable perspective. Those who reject it essentially do so for the same reasons.

24. Question:
"How did the Fall affect humanity?"

Answer: "Just as through one man sin entered into the world, and death through sin, and so sin spread through all men" (Romans 5:12). The effects of the Fall are numerous and far reaching. Sin has affected every aspect of our being. It has affected our lives on earth and our eternal destiny.

One of the immediate effects of the Fall is that mankind was separated from God. In the Garden of Eden, Adam and Eve had perfect communion and fellowship with God. When they rebelled against Him, that fellowship was broken. They became aware of their sin and were ashamed before Him. They hid from Him (Genesis 3:8-10), and man has been hiding from God ever since. Only through Christ can that fellowship be restored, because in Him we have become as righteous and sinless in God's eyes as Adam and Eve were before they sinned. "God made him who had no sin to be sin for us, so that in him we might become the righteousness of God" (2 Corinthians 5:21).

Because of the Fall, death became a reality, and all creation was subject to it. All men die (with the exception of Enoch and Elijah, whom God miraculously took to heaven without death), all animals die, all plant life dies. The "whole creation groans" (Romans 8:22), waiting for the time when Christ will return to liberate it from the effects of death. Because of sin, death is an inescapable reality and no one is immune. "For the wages of sin is death, but the gift of God is eternal life in Christ Jesus our Lord" (Romans 6:23). Worse still, we not only die, but if we die without Christ, we experience eternal death. Another effect of the Fall is that humans have lost sight of the purpose for which they were created. Man's chief end and highest purpose in life is to glorify God and enjoy Him forever (Romans 11:36; 1 Corinthians 6:20; 1 Corinthians 10:31; Psalm 86:9). Hence, love to God is the core of all morality and goodness. The opposite is the choice of self as supreme. Selfishness is the essence of the Fall, and what follows are all other crimes against God. In all ways sin is a turning in upon oneself, which is confirmed in how we live our lives. We call attention to ourselves and to our good qualities and accomplishments. We minimize our shortcomings. We seek special favors and opportunities in life, wanting an extra edge that no one else has. We display vigilance to our own wants and needs, while we ignore those of others. In short, we place ourselves upon the throne of our lives, usurping the role that belongs to God.

When Adam chose to rebel against his Creator, he lost his innocence, incurred the penalty of physical and spiritual death, and his mind was darkened by sin, as are the minds of his successors. The Apostle Paul said of pagan minds, "Since they do not think it worthwhile to retain the knowledge of God, He gave them over to a depraved mind" (Romans 1:28). He told the Corinthians that "the god of this age has blinded the minds of unbelievers so that they cannot see the light of the Gospel of the glory of Christ, who is the image of God" (2 Corinthians 4:4). Jesus said, "I have come into the world as a light so that no one who believes in me should stay in darkness" (John 12:46). Paul reminded the Ephesians, "You were once in darkness but now you are in the light of the Lord" (Ephesians 5:8). The purpose of salvation is "to open the eyes [of unbelievers] and turn them from darkness to light, and from the power of Satan to God" (Acts 26:18).

The Fall produced in humans a state of depravity. Paul spoke of those "whose consciences are seared" (1 Timothy 4:2) and those whose minds are spiritually darkened as a result of rejecting the truth (Romans 1:21). In this state of depravity, man is utterly incapable of doing or choosing that which is acceptable to God, apart from divine grace. "The sinful mind is hostile to God. It does not submit to God's law, nor can it do so" (Romans 8:7).

Without the supernatural regeneration by the Holy Spirit, all men would remain in the fallen state of sin. But thanks to His grace, mercy and loving-kindness, God sent His Son to die on the cross and take the penalty of our sin, reconciling us to God and making eternal life with Him possible. What was lost at the Fall is reclaimed at the Cross.

25. Question:
"What is the guff?"

Answer: The guff is a term the Talmud uses to refer to the repository of all unborn souls. The Talmud is the Jewish commentary on the Torah, or the Old Testament, and especially the first five books of the Bible known as the Pentateuch. Jewish tradition states that the Talmud began as oral teachings handed down from Moses that were eventually completed sometime between the 4th and 2nd century B.C.

Literally, the word guff means "body." The Talmud essentially says, "The Messiah will not arrive until there are no more souls in the guff." The Talmud is saying that there are a certain number of souls in heaven waiting to be born. Until they are born, they wait in a heavenly repository called "the guff," and the Messiah will not arrive until every single one of these souls has been born into the physical world.

Is the idea of the guff biblical? No, it is not. Neither the Hebrew Scriptures nor the New Testament teaches that there is a storehouse of souls in heaven. The Bible does not teach that souls are waiting to be attached to bodies when people are born. The Bible is not explicitly clear on when/how human souls are created, but the concept of the guff does not agree with what the Bible does teach about the origin of the soul. It is far more biblical to hold that God creates each human soul at the moment of conception, or that the human soul is generated along with the body through the physical-spiritual union of conception.

26. Question:
"What does the Bible say about ethnocentrism?"

Answer: Ethnocentrism is the belief that a particular race or ethnic group is superior to all others and all other races and ethnic groups are to be subjectively measured in relation to that race or ethnic group. It is a system of belief that leads to extreme pride and lack of concern for others. Simply put, ethnocentrism is another name for racism, which has been a plague on humanity for centuries and the cause of the death of millions. There is no place among God's people for the ethnocentric attitudes which lead to racism. Such attitudes are contrary to Scripture and displeasing to God.

Biblically, ethnocentrism is sin. All men and women are made in the image of God (Genesis 1:26-27, 9:6), although that image is corrupted by sin. It is because we are created in His image that God does not show partiality or favoritism (Deuteronomy 10:17; Acts 10:34). Jesus did not lay down His life for a particular race of people, but by His death He "purchased men for God from every tribe and language and people and nation" (Revelation 5:9). The Israelites were ethnocentric by virtue of being God's chosen people, but His choice was not based on their merit, but on His mercy and grace. The Scriptures tell us that Jesus came to save the world, both Jews and Gentiles. Paul bears this out by saying, "There is neither Jew nor Greek, slave nor free, male nor female, for you are all one in Christ Jesus" (Galatians 3:28) and "there is no Greek or Jew, circumcised or uncircumcised, barbarian,

Scythian, slave or free, but Christ is all, and is in all" (Colossians 3:11).

Jesus destroyed all barriers of race and ethnicity with His death on the cross. As Paul said in Ephesians 2:14, "For he himself is our peace, who has made the two one and has destroyed the barrier, the dividing wall of hostility." Ethnocentrism, whether based on historical grudges or on the erroneous teachings of men, is wholly contrary to God's Word. We are commanded to love one another as He has loved us (John 13:34), and such a command precludes any discrimination based on race or culture.

27. Question:
"What was the mark that God put on Cain (Genesis 4:15)?"

Answer: After Cain killed his brother Abel, God declared to Cain, "Now you are under a curse and driven from the ground, which opened its mouth to receive your brother's blood from your hand. When you work the ground, it will no longer yield its crops for you. You will be a restless wanderer on the earth" (Genesis 4:11-12). In response, Cain lamented, "My punishment is more than I can bear. Today you are driving me from the land, and I will be hidden from your presence; I will be a restless wanderer on the earth, and whoever finds me will kill me" (Genesis 4:13-14). God responded, "Not so; if anyone kills Cain, he will suffer vengeance seven times over." Then the Lord put a mark on Cain so that no one who found him would kill him" (Genesis 4:15-16). What was this "mark" that God put on Cain to prevent vengeance from being taken against Cain?

The nature of the mark on Cain has been the subject of much debate and speculation. The Hebrew word translated "mark" is 'owth and refers to a mark, sign, or token. Elsewhere in the Hebrew Scriptures, 'owth is used 79 times and is most frequently translated as "sign."

So, the Hebrew word does not identify the exact nature of the mark God put on Cain. Whatever it was, it was a sign/indicator that Cain was not to be killed. Some propose that the mark was a scar, or some kind of tattoo. Whatever the case, the precise nature of the mark is not the focus of the passage. The focus of the passage is that God would not allow people to take vengeance against Cain. Whatever the mark on Cain was, it served this purpose.

In the past, many believed the mark on Cain to be dark skin, that God changed the color of Cain's skin to black in order to identify him. With the corresponding curse that Cain received, the belief that the mark was black skin caused many to believe that people of black skin were cursed. Many used the mark of Cain as an excuse for the African slave trade and discrimination against people with black/dark skin. This interpretation of the mark of Cain is completely unbiblical. Nowhere in the Hebrew Scriptures is 'owth used to refer to skin color. The curse on Cain in Genesis chapter 4 was on Cain himself. Nothing is said of Cain's curse being passed on to his descendants. There is absolutely no biblical basis to claim that Cain's descendants had dark skin. Further, unless one of Noah's sons' wives was a descendant of Cain (possible but unlikely), Cain's line was terminated by the Flood.

What was the mark that God put on Cain? The Bible does not specifically say. The meaning of the mark, that Cain was not to be killed, was more important than the nature of the mark itself. Whatever the mark on Cain was, it had no connection to skin color or a curse on the descendants of Cain. To use the mark on Cain as an excuse for racism and discrimination is blatantly and absolutely unbiblical.

28. Question:
"Who are the people of God?"

Answer: The phrase "the people of God" always indicates a clear relationship. God called Abram (later Abraham) in Genesis 12 to leave his land for a new one that God would show him. Once Abram was there, God says in Genesis 12:2, "I will make you into a great nation and I will bless you; I will make your name great, and you will be a blessing." This nation would become the nation of Israel, the first to be designated as God's people.

God says to Israel through the prophet Isaiah, "I have put my words in your mouth and covered you with the shadow of my hand—I who set the heavens in place, who laid the foundations of the earth, and who says to Zion, 'You are my people'" (Isaiah 51:16). God also confirms Israel as His people in Ezekiel 38:14 in a prophecy to the neighboring nation of Gog.

Are non-Jewish believers in a Jewish Messiah (Jesus Christ) considered the people of God? Yes. Jesus came for all mankind, not just to save Israel (Romans 1:16, 10:12; Galatians 3:28). The relationship of God to His people isn't just Him calling someone His people; they must also call Him their God. Clearly speaking of Israel, the author of 1 Chronicles says, "I know, my God, that you test the heart and are pleased with integrity. All these things have I given willingly and with honest intent. And now I have seen with joy how willingly your people who are here have given to you" (1 Chronicles 29:17). Here, God's people are identified more by their willingness to give themselves to Him than by their nationality.

Anyone who accepts Jesus Christ as Savior and Lord becomes a part of the people of God. It doesn't come through church attendance or good deeds. It is a deliberate choice to follow God alone. That's why 2 Corinthian 6:16 and Mark 8:38 both indicate that a choice has to be made. And when we make that choice to embrace God, He embraces us as well. Then we truly are His people.

29. Question:
"What does it mean to be a part of the family of God?"

Answer: The Bible teaches that Jesus Christ and the Father are One (John 1:1-4), and that He is also the only begotten Son of God (Hebrews 1:1-4). This familial term indicates God regards Jesus as a family member. Born-again believers are told that we, too, are members of this family (Romans 9:8; 1 John 3:1-2). How do we become a part of this family of God? When we hear the gospel, confess our sins, and place our faith and trust in Jesus Christ, we are at that moment born into God's kingdom as His children and become heirs with Him for eternity (Romans 8:14-17).

While Jesus Christ is referred to as the only begotten Son of God, believers are referred to as children born into God's family who need to grow and mature in our faith (Ephesians 4:11-16), and as sons and heirs adopted into His family (Galatians 4:4-7). God's infinite grace and mercy are revealed in Ephesians 1:5-6, which says He redeems sinners, whom He has "adopted as his sons through Jesus Christ, in accordance with his pleasure and will—to the praise of his glorious grace, which he has freely given us in the One he loves."

As children of God, what do we inherit? Nothing less than the kingdom of God (Matthew 25:34; 1 Thessalonians 2:12; Hebrews 12:28)! Ephesians 1:3 tells us that believers are blessed with every spiritual blessing in the heavenly places in Christ. These spiritual blessings are infinite, eternal, and reside in Christ, and by God's grace we are given these blessings as His children. As earthly children we eventually inherit what our parents leave behind for us after their death. But in God's case believers are already reaping the rewards of our inheritance by having peace with Him through the sacrifice of His Son on the cross.

Other rewards of our inheritance include the gift of the indwelling of the Holy Spirit at the moment we believe in Christ (Ephesians 1:13-14) which empowers us to live for Him in the present, and the knowledge that our salvation is secure for eternity (Hebrews 7:24-25).

Being a part of the family of God is the greatest blessing bestowed upon believers and one that should drive us to our knees in humble adoration. We can never do anything to deserve it for it is His gift of love, mercy and grace to us, yet, we are called to become sons and daughters of the Living God (Romans 9:25-26). May we all respond in faith to His invitation!

30. Question:
"What is human nature? What does the Bible say about human nature?"

Answer: Human nature is that which makes us distinctly human. Our nature is distinct from the animals and the rest of creation in that we can think and feel. One of the chief distinctions between human beings and the rest of creation lies in our ability to reason. No other creature has this ability, and there's no question that this is a unique gift bestowed by God. What is unique about this is that it enables us to reflect on our own nature, the nature of God, and from that to derive knowledge of God's will for His creation. No other part of God's creation has a nature capable of doing so.

The Bible teaches that God created human beings in His image. To be in God's image is part of our nature. This means that He enables us to have some understanding of Him and of His vast and complex design. Our human nature also reflects some of God's attributes, although those are limited and, unlike Him, finite. We love because we are made in the image of the God who is love (1 John 4:16). Because we are created in His image, we reflect His nature, and we can be compassionate, faithful, truthful, kind, patient, and just, although these attributes are distorted by sin, which still resides in our nature.

Originally, human nature was perfect by virtue of having been created so by God. The Bible teaches that human beings were created "very good" by a loving God (Genesis 1:31), but that goodness was marred by the sin of Adam and Eve and, subsequently, the entire human race fell victim to the sin nature. The good news is that at the moment of conversion, the Christian receives a new nature. Second Corinthians 5:17 tells us, "Therefore, if anyone is in Christ, he is a new creation; the old has gone, the new has come!" Sanctification, on the other hand, is the process by which God develops our new nature, enabling us to grow into more holiness through time. This is a continuous process with many victories and defeats as the new nature battles with the "tent" (2 Corinthians 5:4) in which it resides— the old man, old nature, the flesh. Not until we are glorified in God's presence will our new nature be set free to live for eternity in the presence of the God in whose image we are created.

31. Question:
"What is the cause of all the anti-Semitism in the world?"

Answer: Why does the world hate the Jews? Why is anti-Semitism so rampant in so many different nations? What is so bad about the Jews? History has shown that at various time over the last 1,700 years the Jews have been expelled from over 80 different countries. Historians and experts have concluded there are at least six different reasons:

• *Racial Theory*–the Jews are hated because they are an inferior race.

Hard Questions About Humanity

• *Economic Theory* – the Jews are hated because they possess too much wealth and power.

• *Outsiders Theory* – the Jews are hated because they are different from everyone else.

• *Scapegoat Theory* – the Jews are hated because they are the cause for all the world's problems.

• *Deicide Theory* – the Jews are hated because they killed our Lord and Savior Jesus Christ.

• *Chosen People Theory* – the Jews are hated because they arrogantly declare they are the "chosen ones of God."

Though these six reasons have been determined to be the major causes of hatred of the Jews throughout the world and history, is there really any substance to them?

• With respect to the racial theory, the truth is that the Jews are not a race. Anyone in the world of any color, creed or race can become a Jew.

• The economic theory citing that the Jews are wealthy doesn't hold much weight. History has shown that during the 17th through the 20th centuries, especially in Poland and Russia, the Jews were desperately poor and had very little, if any, influence in business or political systems.

• As for the outsiders' theory, during the 18th century, the Jews desperately tried to assimilate with the rest of Europe. As outsiders or foreigners, they had hoped that the anti-Semitism would disappear. However, they were hated even more by those who claimed the Jews would infect their race with inferior genes. This was especially true in Germany prior to World War II.

• As to the scapegoat theory, the fact of the matter is that regardless of what group is hated, they will be considered a scapegoat for all the world's evils and ills. The point is that the Jews have always been hated, which makes them a very convenient target.

• As to deicide, the Bible makes it clear that the Romans were the ones who actually killed Jesus, though the Jews acted as accomplices. It wasn't until a few hundred years later that the Jews were cited as the murderers of Jesus. One wonders why the Romans are not the ones hated. Jesus Himself forgave the Jews (Luke 23:34). Even the Vatican absolved the Jews of His death in 1963. Nevertheless, neither statement has diminished anti-Semitism.

• As for their claim to being the "chosen people of God," the Jews in Germany rejected their "chosen-ness" status during the later part of the 19th century in order to be assimilated into the German culture. Nevertheless, they suffered the Holocaust. Today, some Christians and Muslims claim to be the "chosen people" of God, yet for the most part, the world tolerates them and still hates the Jews.

So, this brings us to the real reason by the world hates the Jews. The Apostle Paul tells us: "For I could wish that I myself were cursed and cut off from Christ for the sake of my brothers, those of my own race, the people of Israel. Theirs is the adoption as sons; theirs the divine glory, the covenants, the receiving of the law, the temple worship and the promises. Theirs are the patriarchs, and from them is traced the human ancestry of Christ, who is God over all, forever praised!" (Romans 9:3-5). The truth is that the world hates the Jews because the world hates God. The Jews were God's firstborn, His chosen people (Deuteronomy 14:2). Through the Jewish patriarchs, the prophets, and the temple, God used the Jews to bring forth His Word, the Law, and morality to a world of sin. He sent forth His son, Jesus the Christ, in a Jewish body to redeem the world of sin. Satan, the prince of the earth (John 14:30; Ephesians 2:2) has permeated the minds of man with his hated of the Jews, God's chosen people, because it is through this royal bloodline that His Son, Jesus Christ came and will return again.

Satan tried through the Babylonians, the Persians, the Assyrians, the Egyptians, the Hittites, and the Nazis in an attempt to wipe out the Jews. But he's failed time and time again. God is not finished with Israel. Romans 11:26 tells us that someday all Israel will be saved, and this cannot come to pass if Israel no longer exists. Therefore, God will preserve the Jews for the future, just as He has preserved their remnant throughout history, until His final plan comes to pass. Nothing can thwart God's plan for Israel and the Jewish people.

32. Question:
"What is the breath of life?"

Answer: The climactic height of God's creative work was His extraordinary creation of man. "The LORD God formed the man from the dust of the ground and breathed into his nostrils the breath of life, and the man became a living being" (Genesis 2:7). The supreme Creator of all the heavens and the earth did two things in creating man. First, He formed him from the very dust of the ground and secondly, He did something to distinguish man from His other creatures—He breathed His own breath into the nostrils of Adam.

We learn three significant facts from this one succinct passage in Genesis. First is that God and God alone created man. Man did not evolve from other creatures. Impersonal forces did not form man. All the cells, DNA, atoms, molecules, hydrogen, protons, neutrons, or electrons did not create man. These are only the substances that make up man's physical body. The Lord God formed man. The Lord God created the substances and then He used them to create man. Man was created and formed by God and by God alone.

The word "formed" comes from the Hebrew yatsar which means to mold, shape, form. It pictures a potter who envisions within his mind what he wants to create. This potter has not only the intelligence, but also the power to form his creation. God, then, is the Master Potter who had the image of man within His mind, as well as the power and the intelligence to create man. God had both the omniscience (all knowledge) and the omnipotence (all power) to do exactly what He wanted.

Secondly, God breathed His own breath of life into man. Man is more than dust or physical substance. Man is spirit. We can picture it this way. Man had just been formed by God from the dust of the earth, just a human body lying upon the ground—never having breathed. Then God leaned over and breathed His own breath into the man's nostrils; God breathed into man His own Spirit. This means that God has connected Himself to man in the most intimate way possible. Man is related to God and has the same breath as God, the breath of life.

Thirdly, Genesis 2:7 tells us that man became a living soul (KJV). The word "soul" in Hebrew is nephesh meaning an "animated, breathing, conscious, and living being." It does not mean the spirit of man. It does mean that he was a living soul just like all the other creatures of earth. However, there was one distinctive difference between the animals and man: man was given the very breath of God Himself, the very Spirit and life of God. Man did not become a living soul until God breathed His Spirit and life into man. As both an animate and spiritual being, man is the only living spirit upon the earth, which makes him unique among all living things.

So what is the breath of God? It is the Spirit of God, given to man to animate him both physically and spiritually. The Hebrew word for spirit is ruach which means wind, breath, air, spirit. Further, the breath of God is the life of God. And the life of God is life that lives on and on, the power to live eternally. God's breath is not temporal; the breath of God lives forever. As such, we, the recipients of the breath of life, will live eternally. The only question is where will we live?

Indeed, God has breathed His Spirit into each one of us. Doesn't it make sense then, that our spirit should breathe after God (Psalm 42:1), that we should long for Him with every breath? For as Jesus, our Lord and our Savior, has promised to all those who believe and call upon His name (Jeremiah 29:11-13): "Blessed are those who hunger and thirst for righteousness, for they will be filled" (Matthew 5:6).

of guilt when we violate it and feelings of pleasure and well-being when our actions, thoughts and words are in conformity to our value systems. The Greek word translated "conscience" in all New Testament references is suneidēsis, meaning moral awareness or moral consciousness. The reaction of the conscience occurs when there is an awareness that one's actions, thoughts, and words conform to, or are contrary to, a standard of right and wrong.

There is no Hebrew term in the Old Testament which is equivalent to suneidēsis in the New Testament. The lack of a Hebrew word for conscience may be due to the Jewish worldview, which was communal rather than individual. The Hebrew's consciousness was of himself as a member of a covenant community which related to God and His laws as a group, rather than an autonomous self-awareness between an individual and his God or his world. In other words, the Hebrew was confident in his own position before God if the Hebrew nation as a whole was in good fellowship with Him.

The New Testament concept of conscience is more individual in nature and is seen in three major areas. First, conscience is a God-given capacity for human beings to exercise self-evaluation and critique. Paul refers several times to his own conscience as being "good" or "clear" (Acts 23:1, 24:16; 1 Corinthians 4:4). This tells us that Paul examined his own words and deeds and found them to be in accordance with his morals and value system which were, of course, based on God's standards. His conscience verified that they were in accord with those standards and were, therefore, blameless.

Second, in the New Testament conscience is consistently portrayed as a witness to something. Paul refers to the Gentiles as having consciences that bear witness to the presence of the law of God written on their hearts, even though they did not have the Mosaic Law (Romans 2:14-15). He also appeals to his own conscience as a witness that he speaks the truth (Romans 9:1), that he has conducted himself in holiness and sincerity in his dealings with men (2 Corinthians 1:12), and that his conscience tells him his actions are apparent to both God and the witness of other men's consciences (2 Corinthians 5:11).

Third, conscience is portrayed as a servant of the individual's value system. An immature or weak value system produces a weak conscience, while a fully informed value system produces a strong sense of right and wrong. In the Christian life, one's conscience can be driven by an inadequate understanding of scriptural truths and can produce feelings of guilt and shame disproportionate to the issues at hand. Maturing in the faith strengthens the conscience and applies its promptings to issues of greater consequence in the Christian life.

This last function of the conscience is the issue Paul addresses to the Corinthian church regarding the issue of eating food that had been sacrificed to idols. He makes the case that since idols are not real gods, food sacrificed to them is nothing. But some in the church were weak in their understanding and believed that such gods really existed. Eating food that had been sacrificed to the gods would have horrified them because their consciences were formed by the erroneous prejudices and superstitious views that often accompany spiritual immaturity. Therefore, Paul encourages those more mature in their understanding not to exercise their freedom to eat if it would cause the consciences of their weaker brothers to condemn their actions. The lesson here is that if our consciences are clear because of mature faith and understanding, we are not to cause those with weaker consciences to stumble by exercising the freedom that comes with a stronger conscience.

Another reference to conscience in the New Testament is to a conscience that is "seared" or rendered insensitive as though it had been cauterized with a hot iron and hardened and calloused, no longer feeling anything (1 Timothy 4:1-2). Those with a seared conscience are those who no longer listen to its promptings, who can sin with abandon, delude themselves into thinking all is well with their souls, and treat others insensitively and without compassion.

As Christians, we are to keep our consciences clear by obeying God and keeping our relationship with Him in good standing. We do this by the steady application of His Word, renewing and softening our hearts continually. This also enables us to tread carefully around those whose consciences are weak, treating them with Christian love and compassion.

33. Question:
"What does it mean to believe in the sanctity of life?"

Answer: The phrase "sanctity of life" reflects the belief that because people are made in God's image (Genesis 1:26), human life has an inherently sacred attribute that should be protected and respected at all times. While God gave humanity the authority to kill and eat other forms of life (Genesis 9:3), the murdering of other human beings is expressly forbidden, with the penalty being death (Genesis 9:6).

Humanity was created in God's image, but sin has corrupted that image. There is nothing inherently sacred in fallen man. The sanctity of human life is not due to the fact that we are such wonderful and good beings. The only reason the sanctity of life applies to humanity is the fact that God created us in His image and set us apart for all other forms of life. Although that image has indeed been marred by sin, His image is still present in humanity. We are like God, and that likeness means that human life is always to be treated with dignity and respect.

The sanctity of life means that humanity is more sacred than the rest of creation. Human life is not holy in the same sense that God is holy. Only God is holy in and of Himself. Human life is only holy in the sense of being "set apart" from all other life created by God. Many apply the sanctity of life to issues like abortion and euthanasia, and while it definitely applies to those issues, it applies to much more. The sanctity of life should motivate us to combat all forms of evil and injustice that are perpetuated against human life. Violence, abuse, oppression, human trafficking, and many other evils are also violations of the sanctity of life.

Beyond the sanctity of life, there is a much better argument against these things: the greatest commandments. In Matthew 22:37-39 Jesus says, "'You shall love the Lord your God with all your heart, and with all your soul, and with all your mind.' This is the great and foremost commandment. The second is like it, 'You shall love your neighbor as yourself.'" In these commandments, we see that our actions are to be motivated by love for God and love for others. If we love God, we will value our own lives as part of God's plan, to do His will until it comes about that His will is better served by our deaths. And we will love and care for His people (John 21:15-17). We will see to the needs of the elderly and sick. We will protect others from harm—whether from abortion, euthanasia, human trafficking, or other abuses. While the sanctity of life can be the foundation, love must be the motivation.

34. Question:
"What is Kinism?"

Answer: Kinism is one branch of a diverse series of religious movements that promote racial segregation. This movement is based in Christianity and, for the most part, is populated with people who are historic, Calvinistic, orthodox and Reformed in their doctrinal views. The tendency to adhere to some true doctrines, however, does not mean that Kinists are orthodox in belief and practice. In fact, their adherence to true doctrines, and the extensive theological knowledge of some of the followers of Kinism, makes this legalistic cult all the more dangerous.

It is difficult to get a direct answer about Kinism, because the movement is relatively new and "un-formed" and also because Kinists themselves tend to be quite scholarly and esoteric. But a few things are clear. Unlike the Christian Identity Movement, or the Aryan Nation, Kinists do not believe that non-white races cannot be saved. Also, unlike Anglo-Isrealists, they do not believe that national Israel's true descendents are the British and American people groups.

What makes Kinism different is the belief that God has ordained an order for mankind that goes beyond personal and individual worship. They believe that God has set boundaries for groups of human beings and that human beings should respect those boundaries by maintaining a tribal order. What this means is that you could have a group of white Kinists, and a group of black Kinists, but they would not worship together. They believe that man is usurping God's authority when they "co-habit" with different races, when (as they say) God has ordained a necessary distinction. In the words of one Kinist, "This [belief] affects our ecclesiology since it would consider a multi-racial, drum-banging mega-church to be a foul stench in God's nostrils." Besides being unloving, this assertion is simply un-biblical, promotes a racist point of view, and is a platform for pride and legalism.

Kinists insist on racially segregated churches and communities, and of course, families. They believe that Christians should still adhere to the Old Testament Laws that forbade Jews to intermarry with other tribes / families. They also say that God "separated" the races at the Tower of Babel, and that to "re-integrate" is an affront to the order for mankind that He has ordained. Both of these beliefs, despite having a copious amount of scholarly support in Kinist camps, can be easily dismantled with Scripture.

First, to determine whether Old Testament law regarding segregation plies to the New Testament church, we should ask what the reason for segregation was in the Old Testament. God's reason for this law was very clearly to avoid the introduction / assimilation of pagan idolatry into Jewish society (Malachi 2:11; Deuteronomy 7:3). In the New Testament, with the introduction of the indwelling of the Holy Spirit, and the command to take the good news to the Gentiles, we see a switch from Israel being the only nation acceptable to God, to "any nation that fears Him and does what is right" being acceptable to God (Acts 10:34-35) and is part of the body of Christ. The Kinist will agree with this, saying that any person of any race can be a Christian. But they still say that intermarriage is forbidden, although there is no biblical reason for this.

Though national Israel will be restored to God's favor after the Gentiles have been brought to Him (Romans 11:11-12), the law which says "don't intermarry with foreigners, lest they draw your heart away from God" (Deuteronomy 7:3) is no longer valid because a person could marry a Christian of another race and not be in danger of being drawn away after foreign gods. So, the new command is: "don't intermarry with unbelievers, lest they hinder your walk with God" (2 Corinthians 6:14). Racial segregation is simply no longer necessary, because the church now consists of both Jews and Gentiles who believe in Christ for salvation; in other words, all who have the Spirit are, in a real sense "one brotherhood" (Luke 8:21)

As for God's action at the tower of Babel being taken as His ordaining racial segregation, the story of the Tower of Babel (Genesis 11:1-9) is about God confusing the languages of men so that they would not be able to work together to accomplish evil against Him. It is not about racial segregation. This is proved by Galatians 2:11-14, where Paul opposes Peter for separating himself from the Gentile believers in their church. Another example would be Paul's ordaining as a Christian pastor the Greek-born Timothy (2 Timothy 1:6). He even calls Timothy "my true child in the faith" (1 Timothy 1:2). Timothy's mother was Jewish and a woman of the faith. This implies that Timothy lived and ministered in a community that was both Jewish and Gentile. Did his own mother not attend his church? And, if God wished the races to be segregated, which church would he, being half Jew and half Gentile, be able to pastor? And what about Paul himself, who was a self-proclaimed "preacher, apostle… and teacher of the Gentiles" (1 Timothy 2:7)? If Kinism were true, would not God have sent a Gentile to preach to and teach the Gentiles?

In short, Kinism is simply another attempt to be justified by Law, rather than by the gospel of God's grace. "I am not ashamed of the gospel, because it is the power of God for the salvation of everyone who believes: first for the Jew, then for the Gentile" (Romans 1:16, emphasis added.)

35. Question:
"What is the Christian Identity Movement?"

Answer: The Christian Identity movement is a name that applies to a variety of different religious cults all identified by racist, anti-Semitic principles. These cults are typically found among radically anti-government, extremist right-wing groups and "survival groups." Christian Identity cults are connected by various unbiblical theological similarities, mostly centered on a white supremacist mindset that seeks to replace national Israel with British or American whites as the chosen people of God. This racist theology is followed by over 50,000 people in the United States. The largest Christian Identity Movement group is the infamous Ku Klux Klan.

There are other groups with similar theology to the Christian Identity movement, including British Israelism (the milder philosophy that gave rise to the Christian Identity theology) and Kinism, but Christian Identity is more virulently racist, and there are other differences. Christian Identity followers believe that the end of the world is going to be preceded by a cleansing war, during which all non-whites will be exterminated. This dangerous and scary mindset has given rise to terrorism and other nefarious behavior from Christian Identity followers. The history and activities of the Christian Identity Movement are extensive, but there are two main perversions of Christian doctrine that have led Christian Identity followers to some very wrong conclusions about the world and about God.

First, the Christian Identity movement is famous for the idea that the British (and by extension Americans, Canadians, and others) are the spiritual and literal descendants of the 10 lost tribes of ancient Israel. They believe that the white race now represents God's chosen people, a belief founded in some creative interpretations of migratory history, but not based on fact. The Bible tells us that God will restore Israel, as a nation, to fellowship with Him after protecting them from the many nations that will come against them in the end times. Contrary to the beliefs of the Christian Identity movement, it is clear from this passage that the nation of Israel will be made of the same ethnic people group that was responsible for Christ's death, namely, the Jews (Zechariah 12:10).

The second main unbiblical belief held by Christian Identity followers is that the end times and the return of Christ must be "ushered in" by a genocidal war. Interestingly, this belief fits more closely with the teachings of Islam than of Christianity. The Bible teaches that Christ will return to set up His kingdom without the aid of mankind. The aforementioned passage in Zechariah makes this clear, and it is supported with numerous other passages. Revelation 1:7 says that "all tribes" will witness His coming. Titus 2:3 was written by a Jewish man (Paul) to a Jewish church, as they were all joyfully anticipating Jesus' appearance. There is mention that "wars and rumors of wars" would occur before the end (Matthew 24:6), but there is no indication in Scripture that the Jewish nation would have to first migrate to Northern Europe.

Furthermore, there is no biblical reason to believe that non-white races will ever be eliminated by the hand of God or by His true followers. In fact, the New Jerusalem in Heaven will house all nations, and the kings of the earth will bring the glory and honor of the nations into it (Revelation 21:22-27).

The Lord has always protected the sojourner and the foreigner (Deuteronomy 27:19; Isaiah 56:1-8) and though He commanded Israel not to marry the daughters of foreigners, and so be tempted to worship their idols, He has always drawn, and will continue to draw, converts from other nations, tribes and tongues (Ruth 1:16-17; Revelation 7:9). What distinguishes these converts from those who reject God is not their skin color, but their acceptance of His offer of forgiveness through the shed blood of Christ on the cross. Favor with God is a matter of the heart, not a matter of race or nationality (Galatians 3:28-29).

36. Question:
"What is the flesh?"

Answer: John Knox (c. 1510–1572) was a Scottish clergyman, a leader of the Protestant Reformation, and a man who is considered to be the founder of the Presbyterian denomination in Scotland. Knox has been admired by contemporary theologians as someone who personified a zeal for God, and a commitment to the truth of Scripture and holy living. Yet as he grew close to death, this saint of God admitted his own personal battle with the sin nature he inherited from Adam (Romans 5:12). Knox said, "I know how hard the battle is between the flesh and the spirit under the heavy cross of affliction, when no worldly defense but present death doth appear. I know the grudging and murmuring complaints of the flesh..."

Knox's statement sounds remarkably like that of the Apostle Paul who openly acknowledged a personal struggle with his sin nature: "For we know that the Law is spiritual, but I am of flesh, sold into bondage to sin. For what I am doing, I do not understand; for I am not practicing what I would like to do, but I am doing the very thing I hate. But if I do the very thing I do not want to do, I agree with the Law, confessing that the Law is good. So now, no longer am I the one doing it, but sin which dwells in me. For I know that nothing good dwells in me, that is, in my flesh; for the willing is present in me, but the doing of the good is not. For the good that I want, I do not do, but I practice the very evil that I do not want. But if I am doing the very thing I do not want, I am no longer the one doing it, but sin which dwells in me. I find then the principle that evil is present in me, the one who wants to do well. For I joyfully concur with the law of God in the inner man, but I see a different law in the members of my body, waging war against the law of my mind and making me a prisoner of the law of sin which is in my members. Wretched man that I am! Who will set me free from the body of this death?" (Romans 7:14-24).

Paul states in his letter to the Romans that there was something "in the members" of his body that he calls "my flesh," which produced difficulty in his Christian life and made him a prisoner of sin. Martin Luther, in his preface to the book of Romans, commented on Paul's use of 'flesh' by saying, "Thou must not understand 'flesh,' therefore, as though that only were 'flesh' which is connected with unchastely, but St. Paul uses 'flesh' of the whole man, body, and soul, reason, and all his faculties included, because all that is in him longs and strives after the flesh." Luther's comments spell out that Paul's description of 'flesh' equates to affections and desires that run contrary to God, not only in the area of sexual activity, but in every area of life.

What further light does the Bible shed on the flesh, and how is it defined in Scripture? To get a solid understanding of the term as it is used biblically requires examining its usage and definition in Scripture, how it manifests in the life of both believers and unbelievers, the consequences it produces, and how it can ultimately be overcome.

A Definition of the 'Flesh'

The Greek word for 'flesh' in the New Testament is sarx, a term that can oftentimes in Scripture refer to the physical body of a person. However, A Greek-English Lexicon of the New Testament and Other Early Christian Literature describes the word this way: "the physical body as functioning entity; in Paul's thought esp., all parts of the body constitute a totality known as flesh, which is dominated by sin to such a degree that wherever flesh is, all forms of sin are likewise present, and no good thing can live."

The Bible makes it clear, though, that humanity did not start out this way. The book of Genesis makes it clear that humankind was originally created good and perfect: "Then God said, "Let Us make man in Our image, according to Our likeness . . . God created man in His own image, in the image of God He created him; male and female He created them" (Genesis 1:26-27). Because God is perfect, and because an effect always represents its cause in essence (i.e., a totally good God can only create good things, or as Jesus said, "A good tree cannot produce bad fruit" (Matthew 7:18), both Adam and Eve were created good and without sin. But when Adam and Eve sinned, their nature was corrupted and that nature was passed along to their offspring: "When Adam had lived one hundred and thirty years, he became the father of a son in his own likeness, according to his image, and named him Seth" (Genesis 5:3, emphasis added).

This fact is spoken of many places in Scripture, such as David's declaration in the book of Psalms: "Behold, I was brought forth in iniquity, and in sin my mother conceived me" (Psalm 51:5). David does not mean he was the product of something like an adulterous affair, but that his parents passed along a sin nature to him. In theology, this is sometimes called the "Traducian" (taken from the Latin term 'from a branch') view of human nature, which means a person's soul is created via their parents, with the child inheriting their fallen nature from the process.

The Bible's view of humanity's nature differs from Greek philosophy in that Scripture says the physical and spiritual nature of humankind was originally good. By contrast, philosophers such as Plato saw a dualism or dichotomy in humanity, with such thinking eventually producing a mindset that said the body (the physical) was bad or evil, but a person's spirit was good. This teaching filtered down to groups such as the Gnostics who believed the physical world was mistakenly created by a demi-god called the 'Demiurge'. The Gnostics opposed the doctrine of Christ's incarnation because they believed God would never take on a physical form since the body was evil. The Apostle John encountered a form of this teaching in his day, and warned against it by saying, "Dear friends, do not believe every spirit, but test the spirits to see whether they are from God, because many false prophets have gone out into the world. This is how you can recognize the Spirit of God: Every spirit that acknowledges that Jesus Christ has come in the flesh is from God, but every spirit that does not acknowledge Jesus is not from God" (1 John 4:1-3).

Hard Questions About Humanity

Further, the Gnostics taught that it did not matter what a person did in their body, since the spirit was all that mattered. This Platonic dualism had the same effect back in the first century as it does today—it leads either to asceticism or licentiousness, both of which the Bible condemns (Colossians 2:23; Jude 4).

So contrary to Greek thought, the Bible says that humanity's nature, both the physical and spiritual, were good and yet both were adversely affected by sin. The end result of sin was a nature oftentimes referred to as the 'flesh' in Scripture—something that opposes God and seeks sinful gratification. Pastor Mark Bubek defines the flesh this way: "The flesh is a built-in law of failure, making it impossible for natural man to please or serve God. It is a compulsive inner force inherited from man's fall, which expresses itself in general and specific rebellion against God and His righteousness. The flesh can never be reformed or improved. The only hope for escape from the law of the flesh is its total execution and replacement by a new life in the Lord Jesus Christ."

The Manifestation and Struggle with the Flesh
How does the flesh manifest itself in human beings? The Bible answers the question this way: "Now the deeds of the flesh are evident, which are: immorality, impurity, sensuality, idolatry, sorcery, enmities, strife, jealousy, outbursts of anger, disputes, dissensions, factions, envying, drunkenness, carousing, and things like these, of which I forewarn you, just as I have forewarned you, that those who practice such things will not inherit the kingdom of God" (Galatians 5:19-21).

Examples of the flesh's outworking in the world can be seen in many ways. For example consider a few sad facts taken from a recent survey on the effect of pornography in America. According to the study, every second in the U.S.:

• $3,075.64 is being spent on pornography

• 28,258 Internet users are viewing pornography
• 372 Internet users are typing adult search terms into search engines

And every 39 minutes, a new pornographic video is being created in the United States. Such statistics underscore the statement made by the prophet Jeremiah who mourned that "The heart is more deceitful than all else and is desperately sick; who can understand it?" (Jeremiah 17:9).

The Consequences of the Flesh
The Bible makes it clear that a number of unfortunate consequences occur from living in the flesh. First, Scripture states that those who live according to the flesh, and who never desire change or repent from their sinful behavior, will experience separation from God both in this life and the next:

• "Therefore what benefit were you then deriving from the things [sinful practices] of which you are now ashamed? For the outcome of those things is death."(Romans 6:21)
• "For if you live according to the sinful nature, you will die; but if by the Spirit you put to death the misdeeds of the body, you will live"(Romans 8:13)
• "Do not be deceived, God is not mocked; for whatever a man sows, this he will also reap. For the one who sows to his own flesh will from the flesh reap corruption, but the one who sows to the Spirit will from the Spirit reap eternal life."(Galatians 6:7-8)

Further, a person also becomes a slave to his/her fleshly nature: "Do you not know that when you present yourselves to someone as slaves for obedience, you are slaves of the one whom you obey, either of sin resulting in death, or of obedience resulting in righteousness?" (Romans 6:16). This slavery always concludes in a destructive lifestyle and a deteriorated living, or as the prophet Hosea put it: "For they sow the wind and they reap the whirlwind" (Hosea 8:7).

Hard Questions About Humanity

The fact of the matter is that obeying the flesh always results in breaking God's moral law. Nevertheless, in a very real sense, a person can never break God's moral law, although they can certainly disobey it. For example, a person can climb up on a roof, tie a cape around their neck, leap off the roof in hopes of breaking the law of gravity, and try to fly. However, they will quickly learn that they cannot fly, cannot break the law of gravity, and the only thing they end up breaking in the end is themselves, while proving the law of gravity in the process. The same is true of moral actions: a person may disobey God's moral law through fleshly living, but they will sooner or later only prove the moral law of God true by breaking themselves in some way via their own behavior.

Overcoming the Flesh

The Bible provides a three-step process for overcoming the flesh and restoring oneself to a right relationship with God. The first step is a walk of honesty where a person acknowledges their sinful behavior before God. This involves agreeing with what the Bible says about everyone born of human parents: people are sinners and enter the world in a broken relationship with the God who made them:

- "If You, Lord, should mark iniquities, O Lord, who could stand?" (Psalm 130:3)
- "If we say that we have no sin, we are deceiving ourselves and the truth is not in us. . . . If we say that we have not sinned, we make Him a liar and His word is not in us" (1 John 1:8, 10)

The next step is a walk in the Spirit, which involves calling out to God for salvation and receiving His Holy Spirit that empowers a person to live rightly before God and not obey the flesh's desires. This transformation and new walk of life is spelled out in a number of places in Scripture:

• "I have been crucified with Christ; and it is no longer I who live, but Christ lives in me; and the life which I now live in the flesh I live by faith in the Son of God, who loved me and gave Himself up for me." (Galatians 2:20)
• "Even so consider yourselves to be dead to sin, but alive to God in Christ Jesus."(Romans 6:11)
• "But I say, walk by the Spirit, and you will not carry out the desire of the flesh."(Galatians 5:16)
• "For all of you who were baptized into Christ have clothed yourselves with Christ." (Galatians 3:27)
• "But put on the Lord Jesus Christ, and make no provision for the flesh in regard to its lusts."(Romans 13:14)
• "And do not get drunk with wine, for that is dissipation, but be filled with the Spirit"(Ephesians 5:18)
• "Your word I have treasured in my heart, that I may not sin against you." (Psalm 119:11)

The last step is a walk of death, where the flesh is starved of its desires so that it eventually dies. Even though a person becomes born again through the Spirit of God, he must understand he still possesses the old nature with its desires that wars with the new nature and the desires that come from the Spirit. From a practical standpoint, the Christian purposely avoids feeding the old, fleshly nature and instead practices new behaviors that are driven by the Spirit:

• "But flee from these things [sinful actions], you man of God, and pursue righteousness, godliness, faith, love, perseverance and gentleness" (1 Timothy 6:11)
• "Now flee from youthful lusts" (2 Timothy 2:22)
• "but I discipline my body and make it my slave, so that, after I have preached to others, I myself will not be disqualified." (1 Corinthians 9:27)
• "Therefore consider the members of your earthly body as dead to immorality, impurity, passion, evil desire, and greed, which amounts

to idolatry."(Colossians 3:5)
• "Now those who belong to Christ Jesus have crucified the flesh with its passions and desires."(Galatians 5:24)
• "knowing this, that our old self was crucified with Him, in order that our body of sin might be done away with, so that we would no longer be slaves to sin;"(Romans 6:6)
• "But you did not learn Christ in this way, if indeed you have heard Him and have been taught in Him, just as truth is in Jesus, that, in reference to your former manner of life, you lay aside the old self, which is being corrupted in accordance with the lusts of deceit, and that you be renewed in the spirit of your mind, and put on the new self, which in the likeness of God has been created in righteousness and holiness of the truth."(Ephesians 4:20-24)

Conclusion

Suzanna Wesley, mother to the great preachers and hymn writers John and Charles Wesley, described sin and the flesh this way: "Whatever weakens your reasoning, impairs the tenderness of your conscience, obscures your sense of God, or takes away your relish for spiritual things, in short - if anything increases the authority and the power of the flesh over the Spirit, that to you becomes sin however good it is in itself." One of the goals of the Christian life is the victory of the Spirit over the flesh and a change of life, which manifests in righteous living before God.

Although the struggle will be very real (which the Bible makes clear), Christians have assurance from God that He will bring them eventual success over the flesh, which is a fact that Paul speaks to when he says, "For I am confident of this very thing, that He who began a good work in you will perfect it until the day of Christ Jesus" (Philippians 1:6).

NOW AVAILABLE
from VIP INK PUBLISHING, L.L.C.

The Michael Lewis Story

Author—Michael Lewis
Dreams
ISBN # 978-1939670168

Michael Lewis, team ambassador of the New Orleans Saints, is best known as a return specialist. Although Lewis did not play college football, he was signed by the Louisiana Bayou Beast in 1998. Lewis has also played for the New Orleans Thunder, New Jersey Red Dogs, Philadelphia Eagles, New Orleans Saints and San Francisco 49ers. In 2000, Lewis' life would dramatically change as went from a former Budweiser beer truck driver (thus, the nickname "Beer Man") to being signed by the New Orleans Saints practice squad. In 2001, he was sent by the Saints to play for the Rhein Fire of NFL Europe. Later that year, Lewis would begin his career as a New Orleans Saint. In 2002, he would set an NFL record for combined kick-punt return yardage with 2,432 yards total (1,807 kickoff, 625 punt). He is currently the Saints' all-time career leader in punt returns (142) and punt return yardage (1,482). On June 15, 2007, the Saints released him. The local New Orleans newspaper, the Times-Picayune, titled the news, *"There's a Tear in My Beer"* because he was a local inspiration, who went from beer truck driver to NFL star. Michael Lewis' autobiography covers his life from his humble beginnings to becoming a NFL star. It also covers his faith and determination as well as the struggles he had to face and overcome. His inspiring story will touch the hearts of millions.

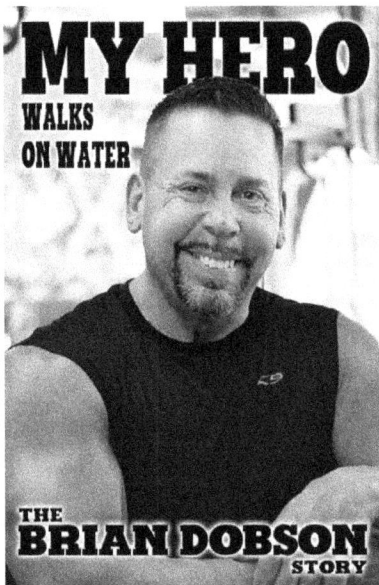

NOW AVAILABLE
from VIP INK PUBLISHING, L.L.C.

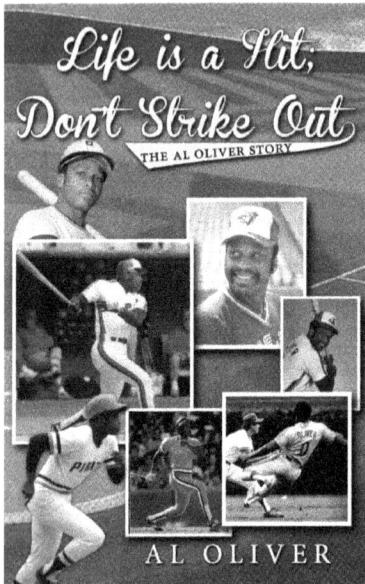

NOW AVAILABLE
from VIP INK PUBLISHING, L.L.C.

Author—Only A Guy
Hard Questions About God—ISBN # 978-0984738205
Hard Questions About Jesus—IBSN # 978-0984738212
The Book Of Prayers—IBSN # 978-0984738229
Hard Questions About The Holy Spirit—ISBN # 978-0984738236
Hard Questions About Heaven And Hell—ISBN # 978-0984738243
Hard Questions About Angeles And Demons—ISBN # 978-0984738267
Hard Questions About Salvation—ISBN # 978-0984738281
Hope In A Lost And Fallen World—ISBN # 978-0984738250
Hard Questions About The End Times—ISBN # 978-1939670007
Hard Questions About Christianity—ISBN # 978-1939670038

Author—Dr. Thomas Moore
Holy Wars: Root Causes
ISBN # 9781939670021

Author—Robert Conners
They Are Real
ISBN # 9780984738298

Author—Stanley Simmons
The Great Deception: Why Are They Here?
ISBN # 9780984738274

www.ingramcontent.com/pod-product-compliance
Lightning Source LLC
Chambersburg PA
CBHW071838020426
42331CB00007B/1772